# WHERE WORDS DEFEAT BULLETS

ASEMANA BOOKS

# WHERE WORDS DEFEAT BULLETS

An Anthology

**Poems for Iranian People and Their 2026 Uprising**

**Compiled by**
**Mansour Noorbakhsh**

ASEMANA BOOKS

Toronto, Canada

FIRST EDITION

Published by ASEMANA BOOKS
ISBN: 978-1-997503-41-5
Book Design: Asemana Books
Cover Art: Asemana Books

To find out more about our authors and books visit: www.asemanabooks.ca

ASEMANA
BOOKS

# WHERE WORDS DEFEAT BULLETS

## Poems for Iranian People and Their 2026 Uprising

*Albert Moritz, Bruce Meyer, Susan Ksiezopolski,*

*Bruce Hunter, Mark McAlister, Olga Stein, Cy Strom,*

*Peta-Gaye Nash, Keith Garebian, Diana Manole,*

*Patrick Connors, Patricia Keeney, Brenda Clews,*

*Brett Campbell, John Oughton, Peter Taylor, Josephine LoRe,*

*I.B. Iskov, Lynn Xu, Hiram Larew, Sylvia Petter,*

*Claudia Piccinno, Emil Nicolae, Josie Di Sciascio-Andrews,*

*Elizabeth Barnes, Elana Wolff, Mahdi Ganjavi,*

*Mbizo Chirasha, Niels Hav, Richard Harrison,*

*EVA Petropoulou Lianou, Antje Stehn, Stephen Kent Roney,*

*PJ Yukon, Kelly Kaur, Chris Wanamaker, Anne Sorbie,*

*George Elliott Clarke*

*And the silent pain of the vine*
*When the little bud*
*Grows at the end of the long, winding branch*

***Ahmad Shamloo***

*Freedom from fear is the freedom*
*I claim for you my motherland!*

***Rabindranath Tagore***

*Freedom*
*Is a strong seed*
*Planted*
*In a great need.*

***Langston Hughes***

# Contents

# Foreword

## Where Words Defeat Bullets

In January 2026, the Iranian regime violently suppressed peaceful protests, shut down the internet and communication networks, and killed and arrested countless civilians—many of them young, educated, and deeply committed to their communities. The depth of this tragedy could be felt when we remember that repressive forces even entered hospitals and killed injured protesters or killed injured protesters in the streets with a second shot.

And it was not the first time that the regime showed its cruelty. In 2022, they shot down flight PS752 and all passengers and the crew perished on this flight. Anytime that Iranian people have raised their voice to demand their rights, the regime has killed the protesters in the street and in the prisons to smother their voice. For five decades, the people of Iran have suffered systematic terror, tyranny, injustice and repression.

Writers, poets, filmmakers, environmental advocates, and other cultural voices have long been targeted, silenced, and murdered by this regime, both in prisons and in their own homes.

Although Iranian writers and poets have been censored, boycotted, persecuted, tortured and killed, they have always fought for freedom of speech and been a strong voice to support human rights.

In response to this violence, poets came together to affirm the power of words, poetry, and collective memory.

Poems live longer than the poets, and remain as a broken thorn under the skin, rekindling instincts for survival. Not only for us in the present time, but also for next generations in the future. These streams of words wash away the dust of toxic lies and oppression and remove the rust of habitual thought. Inspired by poetry, people can no longer ignore - or be forced to ignore - painful loss and chronic destruction. The rain of words flows then, to enlighten what we need to see, and what we need to remember.

A group of poets gathered in North York Public Library, Room 101, on February 15, 2026, from 1 to 3 pm to share their thoughts and words in solidarity with the people of Iran*

The poems in this anthology advocate humanity and human rights and remind us of our rights and our responsibilities as free human beings. As well as the poets who presented their poetry at our gathering, this anthology includes poems by poets who could not attend but submitted their work afterwards.

This is a time of mourning and sorrow, with grief as vast as a nation - a grief even more devastating on account of the shutdown of the internet and telephone. This time, empathy is the balm we can provide, and poetry is the shoulder we can lean on.

In any circumstances whatever the outcome might be, the survivors will need to learn to speak together and find the best way forward. And the work of poets will be one source of inspiration. This passage about dialectics by Plato in the "Phaedrus" dialogue also applies to poets: "Words which can defend both themselves and him who planted them, words which instead of remaining barren contain a seed whence new words grow up in new characters, whereby the seed is vouchsafed immortality, and its possessor the fullest measure of blessedness that man can attain unto."**

I would like to express my appreciation and gratitude to the phenomenal poets who have participated in our poetry gathering and this anthology. In this anthology, first the poems read by the poets in the in-person poetry gathering, and then the poems submitted by other poets are collected in the order they were received. Many thanks to Asemana Books and Dr. Mahdi Ganjavi, without whose efforts this poetry reading session and this book would not happen. And many thanks to all of you, dear friends, who have attended our poetry gathering, and those of you who now have this book in your hands. Together, we feel our hearts full of passion for humanity.

Mansour Noorbakhsh

February 2026, Toronto, Canada

-----------

* You may also watch the video of this gathering at YouTube Link: https://youtu.be/GSVHmeqPHnQ. A few poets who were not present later submitted video and audio recordings,

available at:
https://youtu.be/bVYsbMYAZ70?si=tibb0P_P_ZrrVNZT
** The collected Dialogues of Plato, edited by Edith Hamilton and Huntington Cairns, Prinston University Press, 1962.

# POEMS

# A. F. Moritz

## Poem for the Iranian Uprising 2026

1.

**Powerlessness**

How many times have I written the following
poem?

*O*
*terrible astonishment:*

*I*
 *am*
     *here*
*while the sufferer is*
*there—*

*with me*
*and…*

*but…*

*over there.*

How many more times will I write it?

2.

**Evolution**

Today in the library I came upon
An edition of *Hajji Baba of Ispahan*,
The same one I have—sumptuous, like all those
I got from a toney book club through my Aunt Rose.
Arthur Waley's poems from the Chinese,
Slipcased, with watercolours, with Po Chu-i's
"Chu Ch'en Village", my classic since those days
Of antique boyhood. Another one that stays,
Laurence's *The Seven Pillars of Wisdom*.
Books of the early clash—kinship and schism—
Of Anglo genius and eastern. Orientalism:
Shock, softening to irony, yielding to awe,
The rift of doubt and insight, the final straw
Of certainty...which still has only started
Its work of admitting every broken-hearted
Remorseless assault against greed-and-tyranny's
ranks
Of spears, mercenaries, machine guns, tanks,
Beautifully molded bullets or arrowheads,
In every age where a people starves and bleeds.
"The fire of sorrow has burnt to my heart's core",
Thinking how fifteen hundred skulls or more
Composed each tower of Timur in Ispahan,
Seven centuries back, till that revolt was gone;
How yesterday, maybe today, trucks carry
The body bags to Bagh-e Rezvan cemetery.
While here we are charged with making from our
ease
Some adequate normalcy, some beauty that these

Who now are dead and dying to be free,
To live in justice, can hear of and seem to see
A world kin to their struggle, a good that can be.

3.

**Woman of Persia, Beautiful Naked Poet Murdered**

Like a bird you flew
from the silent prison
and you saw and engrossed
all the fields and mountains under you,
villages and nuclear facilities,
you took in and digested
and became—in in your waist and your hair—
your total country,
laughing with happiness and scorn
at the roses and nightingales, taking in
all the ages, being—and laughing at—the legend,
the land,
of paradise, the garden, the origin
and perfection in dream
of the idea. Never did you hope to return
and never did you return. You flew. Never did you
see again
the streets they dragged you
from and through. You're flying now
but then they smashed you on the floor. I loved,
I was anguished by, I dream of, I stiffened,
alert to the world, at your soft breasts, your lips
that had the outline of a fountain in the woods

in a new land just come to
where our maps and all our travels told us before
that there was no world. They smashed your mouth,
first they cut off your breasts,
they threw you out
before you stank, maybe they shovelled
lime over you, then dirt,
and I never knew, I still don't know
who you were, my lust, my love,
standing naked,
with only your jewels on—you have read
your Baudelaire—and holding
a tablet and a pen,
writing me a letter exposed
to the evening cool
in the open window, feeling
the bared glory of your hips and thighs, absorbed
in the longing of your heart,
for me, who knows you are,
not where you are, not what you are,
not what you are suffering, how you are dying,
my love, obliterated now, and all that I know—
that you are—
so there is truth—
so there is life.

**Albert F. Moritz**, Ph.D. Blake C. Goldring Professor of the Arts and Society Emeritus Victoria University in the University of Toronto Adjunct Professor, Department of English, University of Toronto.
Website: afmoritz.com

# Bruce Meyer

## McLuhan's Canary

Taj texts me as I lie down to sleep.
He says the sunrise over Mumbai
is goldly ancient with muezzin voices,
and his day begins as mine is ending

with moths buzzing on my window,
and the voice of a small world
crying in a dream I must bring to life.
Morning light on the Arabian Sea

is the colour of azaan filling the heart,
calling the world to its singular truth
as I pray that I will wake tomorrow.
The world lives one everlasting dawn

where time is only an illusion.
We no longer dwell in day or night
but in the eternity of a creative mind,
that instant when we think and speak.

It's a small world, my not-so-distant friend,
and we are brothers across beliefs.
A canary sing in a perfumed garden,
and Taj asks if I can hear it.

It sings a daybreak that will not cease,
in a world that cannot stop its turning.
I text him back that I hear the bird,
the song of a planet in search of itself.
Explaining Romanticism to My Daughter

It is always like snow falling in the heart,
and we both turn to stare out the window.

Flakes descend as softly as moonlight,
but in the time it takes to watch the trees

try to catch the broken sky in empty hands,
the wind howls around the house and cries

with the pain and pity of a grieving silence
where the world must be rebuilt for life.

It is the difference between the way snow fell
and what it could tell you of its fall from heaven.

**Bruce Meyer** is the author of 80 books of poetry, short stories, flash fiction, non-fiction, and translations. He was the inaugural Poet Laureate of the City of Barrie. He is a retired professor from Georgian College and the University of Toronto and was a liver transplant recipient in 2022.

# Susan Ksiezopolski

## Under Gods Sun

we are all one
our illusive unity
strengthens our resolve
stitches us into the cause.

To overcome immoral forces
to secure justice for all
unburdened by inequities.

To lead the way out of oppressed mourning
we must graciously carry shadowy struggles
to meet this mountainous moment standing ready
to challenge the rustling rage.

Let us heed the emancipation of refreshing hope
as it rises to extinguish the fire
sparked by rancid words fueling hate
endured for far too long
even the trickle of time cannot silence
it's roaring cry for freedom.

May we join in song to defend the restoration
repair all shattered nations
guided by unseen forces no longer blinded
now redeemed by the forgiveness of past
transgressions.

As we seek allies of reconciliations
even in the blotched benediction of choices

the veil of indifferences lifts
we feel the energy shift
and awaken as sun kissed morning glory.

**Susan Ksiezopolski** an award-winning poet, has published two poetry collections, My Words, and Writing for Change, The Writer's Workbook and Fuel Your Creativity Journal. She is an advocate who explores the intersection of creativity, healing, and mental wellness. A graduate of the Humber School for Writers and founder of WriteWell, she facilitates workshops using writing to build emotional resilience.

# Bruce Hunter

## WHAT MY STUDENTS TEACH ME

Federico
tells me it's too cold here
but some choice.
You go out one morning,
the car hood's open a little;
three sticks of dynamite
and this is the third time.
In El Salvador you take the hint:
you leave.

Ginny Fung
writes of the love
of her and her husband.
The first English she learned
was curses.
Those faces
she could read
in any language.

Cyrous
on the most profound moment of his life
writes a vague tribute
to world harmony and brotherhood.
When I question it,
he says
I am a Baha'i from Iran.
This is for my friends,
not wanting me to seem foolish.
I nod dumbly as he explains

he was made to watch
as the blades fell
and their heads dropped in the street.

Leong Hiu
who now signs her name Lisa
has not seen her brother
since the night
the pirates boarded
in the China Sea,
tells me she likes
the winter here
because when she wakes
all the white stars
are lying on the ground.

Shatha
tells the class
I am visiting my mother after work
babysitting my sister's children
when the sirens went.
We hid under the table
covering my nieces
with our bodies
as the bombs fell
the teapot shattered.
Everything crashing,
it seemed forever.
You were watching that night
She says, on your televisions: Desert Storm.

Dan
says it began in April.

Two million of us sir,
in Tiananmen Square,
I was so proud
to be Chinese.
I was a reporter
when the official
came into the office
and said, no more stories!
I was so angry I quit.
When the tanks came in June
– we ran, hearing the screams,
too scared to look back.
Now I can no longer write,
I study computers.

Fardad
speaks of a trip
to the front with his friend
who asked to drive.
We stopped for water.
I was gone a minute.
When I came out,
a missile, there was nothing left.
At the court martial,
his mother screamed at me,
I should have been in his place.

And me,
what do I know.
I am a man on the beach

**Bruce Hunter**'s award-winning best-selling novel In the Bear's House, his 12th book, was just rereleased

in May by Frontenac House. In 2024, his novel Nella casa dell'orso (In the House of the Bear) was published in Italy by iQdB edizioni. In 2023, his poetry collection Galestro was published in Italy. Bruce's poetry, fiction, reviews, interviews, and creative nonfiction have appeared in over 100 blogs, journals, and anthologies internationally. He is a proud new grandfather to Julian, Alice, Lucas, and wee Theo.
https://share.icloud.com/photos/0e3OYUKpTY60K2yolkfHua5Zw

# Mark McAlister

## Bullets And Words

Bullet
a thing of beauty
        sleek
                silent
                        …impressive!

Barrel
with mechanism
        faultless
                finely tuned
                        a perfect framing!

Finger
the final touch
        quick
                easy
                        the perfect solution!

Word
not much at first
        tubby
                noisy
                        just waddling by

Mouth
mixed purpose
        meandering

often mistaken!

Ego
a trigger in itself
thoughtless
reactive
a troublemaker!

In poems
words are like bullets
beautiful
finely tuned
the perfect touch
not a solution
but a new beginning

**Mark McAlister** grew up in Toronto. After High School, he studied movement and creative speech in Spring Valley, New York. He went on to have a career as a management consultant. He founded Warm Handshakes Inc., organizing business development programs in the tech sector in communities across Ontario. His deep interest in the mystery of human communication was a critical factor in his practice. Now retired, he is devoted to creative writing projects, and to organizing and presenting at Speaking Word events.
He lives with his wife Debbie at Hesperus Village, just north of Toronto.

# Olga Stein

## In Search of Words

You've asked for a poem.
I agreed. Now I struggle
to find words for things we're witnessing.
Nature didn't build us for
looking on pure evil —
the kind of cruelty
that short-circuits thought
and paralyzes the imagination.
There is wickedness that has neither
a beating heart nor other parts
we'd recognize as human.
If only we could name it —
this blackness that swallows light,
depravity that muffles screams—
even when they come in torrents,
or sound waves big enough to 'roll'
over entire cities.

Recall that in Pinochet's Chile,
abductees were murdered and made to disappear.
Pinochet's henchmen used public spaces,
including sports stadiums —
places built for mass celebration of the nation's
brightest flowers,
its most formidable youth.
The Estadio Nacional became a site for torture and
degradation.
How perverse was this assault
on the fragility and dignity of human life

in places meant to showcase the country's
strength, endurance, beauty.
It took years to wash the scent of
suffering from the walls.
But now we know. The world knows.
Rest assured, atrocities won't stay hidden,
despite the blackouts.*

Time is running out, and I still don't
have suitable words—
ones I'd like to offer like water
to ease a dire thirst.
It's like cupping water that seeps through my
fingers,
the same way a dying breath
passes unseen from people shot in streets or
hospitals,
while parents, wives, husbands, and children are left
to grieve,
clutching with trembling fingers
photos, items of clothing, high school
or university diplomas
(testaments to precious youth).
We've witnessed their mourning, despite the
blackouts.

I don't have the words needed
to eulogize the departed, or those
souls still slipping through
the ever-widening cracks in universal justice.
Still, I'd like to honour each one,

recite their names every night before sleep.
There's beauty in these names.
Only I wish I hadn't been called on
to gather them into a dirge and sing:
Bahar, Asal, Adam, Akram, Fatemeh, Leila, Ali,
Shima, Maryam,
Arezou, Elham, Nazanin, Mehran, Niusha, Yazdan,
Parnian,
Sepehr, Sahand, Omid, Mehdi, Shiva, Yousef,
Setareh, Jafar.

I wish to fall asleep not in the dark,
but to the gentle glow of a soft light
that promises another day.
I hope to wake to a sun shining
like a talisman — assuring women and men
yearning for freedom the world over
that freedom is coming.

----------

*During the first few years following Augusto Pinochet's coup and the dictatorship he established in Chile, there was an interrogation centre located on 3037 Irán street in the Macul district of Santiago. This site was known as Venda Sexy (Sexy Blindfold) or La Discothèque. It was one of the most brutal secret detention and torture centers operated by Chile's secret police, the DINA (between 1974 and 1977). Venda Sexy was the name given by the perpetrators because detainees were kept blindfolded at all times and systematically subjected to sexual violence. Inmates

named it La Discothèque because DINA agents
played loud music at all hours to mask the screams
of those being tortured.

**Olga Stein** has a PhD in Canadian literature and cultural studies. She's an editor and essayist. Her first poetry collection, Love Songs: Prayers to Gods, Not Men, was published in July of 2025.

# Cy Strom

Cy Strom, co-editor with Bänoo Zan of Woman Life Freedom: Poems for the Iranian Revolution (Guernica Editions: 2025), asked to read other writers' works. Two poems in Woman Life Freedom were translated by Ali Asadollahi, who was arrested in January 2026; the author of one of these poems, Alireza Adine, was also arrested that same month. Cy read Adine's bloodchilling poem "Our Protests' Reality" and excerpts from Asadollahi's unpublished essay "The Echoes in My Cell: A Witness's Reading of Woman Life Freedom."

Alireza Adine, a poet, writer and visual artist, was born in 1974. In about three decades, he has published five poetry books. Ali Asadollahi, a poet, essayist and translator, is the author of six Persian poetry books; his poems and translations have appeared in numerous US and other publications. Both are active in the Iranian Writers' Association, and both had been arrested as well during the Woman Life Freedom protests. Davood Bayat, a visual artist and poet, is the author of the second poem translated by Ali Asadollahi that appears in the anthology, "The Name." These three brave poets asked to be published under their own names. They have resolved to live openly as free citizens in defiance of a violent dictatorship, and they are not afraid for their names and their thoughts to be known.

In his essay, Ali recalls his time in solitary confinement, "where the world is reduced to four walls and the frantic pulse in your own ears." He weaves into his own lived experience themes that loop through the anthology – its poems and its two essays: reflections on the living power of language and memory, “the echoes of chanted slogans,” lines of poetry as sacrament, as an act of survival. He writes as witness to the volume’s truths, burdened but also liberated by the witness’s moral imperative to tell the whole, complex truth. In that spirit, Ali chose to translate a pair of “seemingly contradictory” poems. Davood Bayat’s “The Name” performs the sacred transfiguration of a name into a “SYMBOL”: the name of the murdered Jina (Mahsa Amini). Davood Bayat’s poem, Ali writes, is the unconquerable soul of the revolution, just as Alireza Adine’s “Our Protests’ Reality” is the revolution’s broken body.

Ali dedicates his essay to his sister, Anisha Asadollahi, imprisoned for her fight for justice and equality.

Many of the poems in Woman Life Freedom are delicate, lyrical, contemplative and picturesque. “Our Protests’ Reality” is not. “Not only blood ... / shit spreads too / after you’re shot.” Alireza Adine’s opening lines shove us through the doors of a kind of mental dissection room into a reeking morgue, a seething death pit. Yet the reality is that we are only a crowd of onlookers on a street somewhere in Iran. A protestor has been shot in the gut. The corpse stinks. It releases ugly noises. People stop and stare; some people laugh. We are caught in a video world, but the regime knows that this video can’t be released. This murder won’t be documented. Witness

falls silent: “More dirty death. / More killed / than they announce.”
Ali Asadollahi writes of Alireza Adine’s poem: “It is a brutal, confrontational piece of anti-poetry,” an act that smashes our belief in “the cheap grace of martyrdom.” It is a poem for terrible times.

# Peta-Gaye Nash

## What lives in your cells

voice of resistance in you and you and you.
light, energy, substance unseen BUT
real as your hand in front of your face

rage of rebellion under 400 years submission
lash, whip, cat o' nine, rubble
of quashed rebellions, rising, uprising

music of resilience wrapped in toil, sweat, heart
ache you feel me, pulsating, drumbeat, screech of
electric guitar
rock n roll, reggae, rap, blues, afro beats,
a song, a speech, a dance

Jonkonnu, Capoeira, Jazz
Elastic, rocking atoms, gyrating seams
Fashion flying, fighting, floating

Rooted and rising
your sweetness satisfying
I can't dance if you don't drum
Can't sway if you don't strum

Quivering strings
Click click clacking maracas
Cymbal clang and tom tom bang

voice, music, rage
Living in you and you and you
real as your hand in front of your face
real as the keyboard, drums and base

Rooted and rising.

## After we heard the news

***After we heard the news of mass unlawful killings, targeting heads and torsos, and cut the Internet to hide their crimes***

Soheila sits at her desk
in cubicle beside mine
crying! My country
can't get in touch
with my brothers
government shut down
the internet.
I hold her hand, thinking
about the Internet, taken
for granted. A right, existing
like free speech, like
posting what I want
mostly anyway

Soheila sits at her desk
in cubicle beside mine
reminiscing! My country
used to be a great
place with freedom
prosperity, human rights
until it was destabilized
by the west.
I hold her hand, thinking
about the west, hearing
one side of the story.
One country, good, saviour, fair

fed to us like Frosted Flakes
Sweet, pretty, poisonous

Soheila sits at her desk
in cubicle beside mine
moaning! My country
thousands massacred,
those who speak out
who protest, arrested,
tortured, even doctors
who treat protesters
I hold her hand, thinking
about protesters, it takes
hot iron courage, it takes
souls willing to die
for dignity for freedom

Soheila sits at her desk
in cubicle beside mine
reflecting! This regime is
Hitleresque.
I hold her hand, thinking
how we cast blame
wondering how they
let it happen
Psych 101 explained
people stand by watching, waiting,
doing as commanded, fearful
mostly anyway

Some grandchild or great
will one day ask why
did everyone allow this massacre

what did you do
I held a hand and listened
I will say feeling ashamed
at the inadequacy
Into questioning eyes
I will say I wrote a poem
feeling ashamed
at the inadequacy.

Soheila in the cubicle beside mine
says, what can we do, what can
anyone do? Thank you for listening.

# Neither Here Nor There

I always knew I didn't belong here
Staid, structured and stringent
Rules designed to control and mold
people into spiritless beings
who follow unquestionably
Mere numbers, joyless
structures of flesh and bone
Death of the mind

I always knew I didn't belong there
Rampant disorder
Reign of chaos and her king corruption
An overgrown jungle
danger lurking at every turn
structureless, survival of the fittest
senseless evil and unparalleled joy
Death of the body

I always knew I belonged neither here nor there
wandering the landscape
unmoored, unsettled
Forever striving for more
Toil takes it's toll and still
home is nowhere

**Peta-Gaye Nash** is a multi-genre writer of adult short fiction, children's literature and poetry. She is known for captivating storytelling, vivid characters and insight into human experience. Her short story collection, Told Ya - Stories is published by Tamarind

Tree Books, 2024 and explores themes of class differences, adversity, endurance, and resilience. Told Ya - Stories won Third Place Fiction in the 2025 Next Generation Indie Book Awards; Distinguished Favorite in the 2025 NYC Big Book Award program; Winner Short Stories Category 2025 Independent Press Award.

# Keith Garebian

## Music for rough tongues

It was thought the heart of the land
would not be afflicted from within,
the Sacred Book decreeing
you lived to dream the past,
nothing to ravage it,
the present with song birds, women
as real as imagination wants,
the future a magical place.

But now is a nightmare, your map
scorching young and old, with tyrants'
biases for false angels with wings
to raise up orthodox obsessions
to a great mosque's glittering minaret
while white wolves of the west
howl at the guarded wall, leaders
of the pack salivate greedy graft.

It is not the night or moon that slays you,
nor the desert, the sea, or the sun.
It is priests shrieking sermons, guards
and rulers with treacherous weapons,
killers of enlightened dreams.

You were born with wounds,
your hands feel stone, salt burning lips,
hearts stung with sharp grief,
your earth not an anthem, not wine
or rainbows, nor all light

on jasmine or swaying palm.

You, the ones who see dark holes
in the heart of your land, throw dice
to risk massacre by ruffians, recite poems
of freedom, your voices falling like feathers
on burning sand, while killers abduct
mirrors, obstinate songs, desolate tunes,
living diaries, desires, stifling what they fear—
the history of earthquakes, lightning,
voices with secrets deep in grains
of your skin, brave bone marrow.

You are the true lovers of homeland,
guardians of hopeful days, voices stigmatic,
martyrs of passion, moons looking
down at wreckage, life shrinking
as tyranny and death
force the moment.

But you know the wilderness
of youth bears gifts, music for rough
tongues, hearts in adamant chains,
as you sing above nightingales,
ambergris breeze, flood tides
of blood. Your linked hands,
embraces, as real as dying,
as real as a storyteller's
tales, the avant-garde
light burning on water near
the city's walls, shadowed
by human shards, many masses dying
free of fear, raising ruined faces.

Praise be to your arms outstretched
to the sun, your unmemorized names
creating an unexpunged anthem,
a chorale with a single rising finale:
Every death is a first death but
biers of the dead make beds for the newborn.

**Keith Garebian** has received plaudits for his twelve poetry collections, especially Children of Ararat, Poetry is Blood, Against Forgetting, and In the Bowl of My Eye. Two of his poems have been set to music, one by American Gregory Spears, the second by Juliet Palmer in Toronto. Garebian recorded 18 of his poems from Poetry is Blood on CD. Garebian has served on juries for the Gerald Lampert and Raymond Souster Awards, and has won many awards and grants, including a writing grant from the Canada Council, and over three dozen from the OAC, and last year Guernica published an anthology of essays about his works.

# Diana Manole

## As a child, I loved the dictator—

In grade two, I proudly donned my military-like uniform,
swearing, hand on the flag—
„*...voi fi credincios poporului şi Partidului Comunist Român...*"
"...I will be faithful to the people and the Romanian Communist Party..."
a communist baptism
a *pioneră* with a red kerchief tight around her neck
like the collar of a puppy, starting the obedience training
radiant in my white shirt, swaying my pleated skirt
in front of the mirror.
That night I went to bed fully dressed,
dreaming I'd be the Pioneer chosen to give *Tovarăşului*
flowers on his birthday, live on national TV.

***

In grade-four Music, I howled hymns, a tone-deaf
but ecstatic member of the nation-wide choir—
„*Partidul, Ceauşescuuuu, Româniaaaa*"
"The Party, Ceauşescu, Romania!"
Each classroom a secular church with
his oak-framed photo the only icon
tribute songs and poems replacing prayers and lullabies.
When I failed the Caudine tuning fork test,

I declared myself a traitor and asked the school's
nurse
to cut out my tongue.

***

In grade-six Russian, the teacher taught us
action and stative verbs
with politically enlightening examples—
*« Товарищ Президент стоит на балконе*
*Дворца Народов. »*
"The Comrade President stands on the
balcony of the Palace of the People."
I planned to run away from home and run to the
palace
to meet *Tovarăşul*—
the prince with gold-crusted work boots
and diamond hammer and sickle
to slice the nation's Promethean liver
keeping the communist flag forever drenched in red
the most handsome comrade ever,
eyes like hot charcoal,
lips like raspberries, voice more soothing than
Dad's.

***

In grade-seven Art, I learned to draw his portrait—
the Father of the People, the nation's only flawless son,
*„Cel mai iubit şi cel mai ascultat."*
"The most beloved and the most obeyed."
each graphite line an IV tube feeding my heart to the regime,
live shreds snatched from millions of child devotees,
encased in the foundations
of each local bastille, each madhouse for the politically insane,
each lavish presidential villa
the shaky sketch, my most prized achievement,
hidden for safekeeping in Mom's dowry chest.

***

When I turned 16, my gift was the Radio Free Europe family secret—
Dad, Mom, and I hiding in the windowless cellar
crouched on burlap bags full of onions and potatoes
*„Nu spune la nimeni că ne bagă la-nchisoare!"* they warned me.
"Don't tell anyone or they'll stick us in jail!"
news sneaking across the Iron Curtain over short waves,
a rusty wire snaking from our little transistor
all the way to the cast iron radiator in the bedroom,
turning it into an antenna
catching glimpses of elusive truths like a butterfly net

truth, as critically endangered as trust and empathy
a raw awakening,
slowly detoxified,
rebaptized in the crowds of
the 1989 anti-communist revolution.

***

Now I watch the news and mourn—
peaceful protests drown in blood to feed vampiric governments,
women defaced with acid by vigilantes granted forgiveness in advance,
bombs blossoming above kindergartens and hospitals,
people seeking freedom legally lashed in the name of God

*Dumnezeul cui?*
Whose God?

so many executioners eager to please—
sleepwalking adults trapped in their leaders' narcissistic dreams,
at-will henchmen ready to live or die
tunnel vision, a pandemic with no cure
so little room for love.

**Note:** This poem was inspired by the thousands of people killed or imprisoned during the peaceful protests that started in Iran on 28 December 2025 and during the 2022-2023 Woman Life Freedom uprising, as well as by the Russian invasion of Ukraine after a kindergarten was hit by a Russian drone on 22 October 2025 in Kharkiv. This is my attempt to increase awareness against mass brainwashing based on my personal experience, growing up in Romania during the communist dictatorship. My gratitude to Heidi Greco and Sonja Greckol, two dear friends and members of the Feminist Caucus of the League of Canadian Poets, who provided detailed feedback and helped me edit this poem.

„Pionierii României“ (Pioneers of Romania, 1945-1990), included all children between 7 and 15 years old to ensure that they knew the communist ideology and participated in its implementation.

## Iran needs us, we need Iranian women

*To Masha Amini and all women martyrs of the fight for freedom*

"Women's rights are human rights!" she gasps
before
everything goes blue.
Blue-skinned girls and women walk, run, dance
on the streets of Tehran
they toss their hijabs in the air, their cerulean
long hair
raining down fire and burning sulfur onto the walls
of Evin prison.
The Persian Bastille implodes,
godless women's guardians and state enforcers turn
into pillars of salt—
whirling mothers, daughters, wives, and sisters
refract joy,
female love to God's love, life to life, freedom to
freedom.

"Killing women is killing the human species," she
gasps
before everything goes dark.
The world at a standstill—
crushed breasts ooze blood instead of colostrum,
bees make venom instead of honey,
suicidal seraphs smash themselves
into the golden-rimmed bulletproof windows of
dictators and forgers of religions
who turn profit from hunger and death.

"Say her name!" she hears in the darkness,

a world-wide awakening,
millions of all ages, races, and religions respond,
chanting her name, pulling her back
into the light.

Writer, translator, and scholar, **Diana Manole** was born in Bucharest, Romania, and in 2000 emigrated to Canada. Her poetry was featured in English and/or in translation in literary magazines in fifteen countries. Manole was nominated for a Pushcart prize and awarded the 2020 Very Small Verse prize of the League of Canadian Poets, Honorable Mention in the 2023 Lush Triumphant Poetry of *subterrain* magazine, and two awards for her translations of Romaian poetry into English. The English-Romanian dual-language "*Praying to a Landed-Immigrant God*" (Grey Borders Books, 2023) is her seventh collection of poems. Since 2013, she has been dreaming and writing poetry in English. You can read more of her work at
https://www.linkedin.com/in/dianamanole/

# Patrick Connors

## Inuit Man Trying to Vote

Tiivi Tullaugak, a high school student
from Ivujivik, Nunavik, wanted to vote
in Canada's Federal Election for the first time.

He went to the local polling station to cast his
ballot. But after waiting several hours, Tiivi
was told the polls would not be opening.

In Salluit, Quebec, about 74 miles from Ivujivik,
also with a largely Inuit population, the polls
closed after only a couple of hours.

How could it be in 2025 that eligible voters in seven
Inuit communities either had difficulties voting
or were unable to vote at all?

Tiivi Tullaugak is a citizen of the nation of Canada.
He is a partner in our shared destiny, and has
a legal right to have his voice heard.

# AI

Artificial Intelligence can't write a good poem.
It does not know when to use alliteration
and how much, or when to pull back.
It can't measure breath by words.
AI does not have soul.

By the time this poem is published
programmers may have fed the machine
Shakespeare and Yeats, Dorothy Livesay
and Maya Angelou, as well as a system
to tell which poems are considered good.

But AI will still not be able to write a good poem.
Because AI never scored a goal or caught a fish.
AI never broke an arm or burst their first pimple.
AI was never betrayed by a friend or a false ideal.
AI has never fallen in love.

Artificial Intelligence
can provide a succinct reply to emails, write
worker reviews with guidelines for advancement
and maybe even take over the world if we let it.
But AI will never write a good poem.

# On an Icy Minneapolis Street

"The Party told you to reject the evidence of your eyes and ears.
It was their final, most essential command." - George Orwell, 1984
Renee Nicole Good was a citizen of the United States.
She was a wife, a mother, a poet, and a human being.

On January 7th, she engaged in civil disobedience.
She idled her car crossways and blocked two lanes.

An ICE agent approached the left front of her car.
She said, "That's fine, dude. I'm not mad at you."

He advanced on her, recording with his cell phone.
She reversed, turning left, as she tried to get away.

If she had been trying to run him over, she would
have turned right in reverse, then turned hard left.

She turned left in reverse to get the open space
to turn right. The ICE agent shot her four times.

He shot her point blank, turned and walked away,
called her a vulgar name for all the world to hear.

On an icy Minneapolis street, in broad daylight,
Renee Nicole Good was murdered in cold blood.

# Dig

The city of Toronto shut down for most of February.
It had been some time since there was so much
snow
all at once, and we didn't know how to deal with it.
Municipal spokespersons said it could take as long
as three weeks to clear all the roads and sidewalks.

Last Thursday I watched one of the greatest games
of hockey I may ever see. But my lasting memory
is of the fans booing each other's national anthems
due to the tactless words of one man. Commercials
reminded of a nearing election called upon this fear.

Two days later were the birthdays of two wonderful
friends. Between celebrations, I learned of the
deaths
of two other friends. One had suffered greatly, while
the other went unexpectedly. I felt so many things
that I didn't know which was the appropriate
feeling.

The strained relationship with our closest ally
and the loss of these dear people have left me
feeling snowbound. I guess all I can do is put
on a heavy jacket, pick up a shovel, and start
to dig my way out - no matter how long it takes.

**Author's Note**:
I thank you for letting me be part of this very special event. These are challenging we live in, and it has become imperative to be on the right side of history. Over 300,000 people were at the rally here on Yonge Street February 14th (the day before Where Words Defeat Bullets). I walk with a cane, and I don't go to rallies these days. However, I unequivocally stand in solidarity with the people of Iran.
While it will likely take a focused effort from an international coalition to defeat the regime, the beautiful people of Iran must be the ones to decide what happens afterwards. For too long, outside interests have compromised their safety and security, as well as their ability to live and grow. Globalist agendas must fade into the background, while the citizens of Iran become the authors of their own destiny!
"Inuit Man Trying to Vote" - there were barriers placed for Inuit wishing to vote in the most recent federal election; "AI" - I am taking revenge on Artificial Intelligence for its inability to write a good poem; "On an Icy Minneapolis Street" - On January 31st, I hosted an event to protest the shooting of Renee Nicole Good. I opened the event by reading this succinct poem.

**Patrick Connors** first chapbook, Scarborough Songs, was released by Lyricalmyrical Press in 2013, and charted on the Toronto Poetry Map.
Along with Asemana Magazine, he has recently been published in Spadina Literary Review, Tower Poetry,

Rabble Review, Paddler Press Spirit Fire Review, and Dissident Voice.

He has performed at the Austin International Poetry Festival; featured in numerous reading series such as The Art Bar, Wild Writers, and Plasticine Poetry; hosted events under the 100,000 Poets for Change banner, as well as the United May Day Committee; and was on the organizing committee for The Great Canadian PoeTrain Tour.

His first full collection, The Other Life, was released in 2021 by Mosaic Press.

His most recent chapbook, Worth the Wait, was released in 2023 by Cactus Press.

His latest collection, The Long Defeat, was released in 2024 by Mosaic Press.

Facebook:

https://www.facebook.com/patrick.j.connors.3

Instagram: https://www.instagram.com/patjtconnors/

Twitter: https://twitter.com/81912CON

# Patricia Keeney

## Out of Iran

Suddenly Tehran.  Gripping the neck. Flattening
hair. Strangling. Pulling. Tugging. Fidgeting. A
bounding woman bound.

I am so wrong…here. Who is wrong? What is right?
Here.

At the bazaar with Mirza. Snaky halls, scented
stalls, robes and hands. Long gauzy scarf. Old
Persia woven in. Attempting fashion. Collapsing
like a tent in hot wind. Silky black square slip/
slides off the curling novice nun I never was. Gentle
scarf seller smiles indulgently.
-I can't keep it on.
-Takes time.

Shamed by black-eyed lush-lipped beauties, cloth
coyly draped to hide shape because god is a man.
Standing in the hotel lobby trying to neutralize
colour, cover flesh, annihilate flair. Aware it is not
the men who look. It is the women whose disguise I
compromise. Who get arrested for high stepping
leather boots.

Hair clips amuse them, tracking wayward waves.
Mirza lends soft hued pashminas to settle me.     -
No you don't need the hijab. That's professional.

The professional women of Iran.

Six hundred years ago, a woman played dulcimer. Rich brown curls tumbling down. Resplendent in velvet rose and stitched pearl, she makes a music I can't hear.

Mirza drives below mountains of snow between creamy concrete boxes in rows. Sun sparkled. Quiet and close, her own snug plot rises on narrow stairs windowed all the way up. Small, her place creates space, opening unexpectedly. A bed in the wall. Couch and desk and sweets with lime. Wedding photos. Satin and lace. Another self mincing in strappy sandals, hair swept up. Diaphanous sundress clinging.

From past to present. Clinging.

Jars and cups and painted vessels full of wine. None now. Nor closeness of the face. Nor languid touch where blossoms blow and latticed wind through fluted terrace goes. Nor pointing painted toes. Nor feeling all the fabrics of design against soft skin, nature's every outline, coloured in.

Paradise then. Persian garden of delights.

Yesterday was hers. Today is what she has.

The Shah's Parisian glitz turned shabby Soviet.
Concrete bunkers for hotels.
-I remember it elegant, shyly, she confides
-when I was a schoolgirl.

It is dangerous to remember. And necessary.

Shining domes circle. Their tendrils and stars glow lemon and lime. Dangerous to look.

When trouble breaks, she keeps saying revolution instead of demonstration.
-A Freudian slip?
Definitely.

*

I'm here at the Fajr Theatre Festival to see drama. But it's all on the streets where cell phones go dead. And we're hurried from crowds. Where our translator's friend is gunned down, because (runs the story) he looked like police and was mobbed.

So muted on stage. Veiled and distant. Crackling Attic tragedy rigged and strung up for fierce masters, fanning the clerical flames.

News from the badlands. Rogue troupe performing something dangerous. Long ugly taxi ride south of the city. Chasing beauty through bloody slaughter. Orphaned Afghan youths and angry street slogans. Whoever does the mothering owns the child. Whoever tends the land keeps it.

Two women for three acts talking. While the room fills up with sand. Their mouths, their eyes, their house, their lives – a choking desert dust.

Iranian drama. Intimate writhing twisted to song. A sobbing. A wailing. A soaring. The grand ancient legend shrunk to a puppet. White wisdom of Rumi, head tilted and happy. Whirling to heaven, expecting all ecstasy. Dancing doll on invisible strings.

*

Shops in the street of artisans sell intricate snowflake petals, blue on fragile copper plates. Miniatures of Isfahan. Tiny tiles from heaven. Dishes curved like boats to sail seas of saffron rice. Olives in walnut and pomegranate.
-Enriched, she says. We call them enriched olives.

Shady night town sleeps in eerie ghost light, pale bulbs hissing secrets of '79 in tawdry yellow and green.

-The traffic will kill you, Mirza warns, sprinting ahead of us, hospitably dodging deadly wheels. -Watch out for scooters. Probably police in plain clothes.

-Put away your cameras.

What are we doing wrong?

One of us doesn't, grips a railing, is told to move on, doesn't. South American, he knows the drill.

-Our passports condemn us. British or American and they think we're all spies.

In deeply gouged gutters, full garbage bags wait for collection, wriggling with rats.

*

Inside the folk restaurant, life is good. Stories told with tambour and flute, bouzouki and drum. Cultural sagas writhe in their songs. Wrought male voice pitched high as blindness, arms wide to clap his people close.
-I love you, Canada.

Then, the flat skin drum. Ecstatic hands. Flying as far as our glaring tundra, as deep as the dreams of Darius. Brooding at the edge of explosion, curtain of hair flinging out, whipping back.

*

The most important questions in Mirza's job interview for college teaching are religious. Were you at Friday prayers? What was the Imam's message? She wants to do gender studies and look at plays by women in Iran but her male professors discourage her.
-What about the female academics?
-They are also passed over, cannot publish.

Carefully she checks her camera.
-Why?

-I'm learning photography so I can document the ignored work of women in Iran, such as the hair removal technician or the washer of corpses.

*

Palace of the Shah. Paradise now. Under the glistening mountain, rich green dreams. Glass boutiques, marbly. Balconies opening out, spilling down. Lavish escape routes lacing the slopes. Passports and bribes. Parties and dancing and alcohol. Keys to a kingdom of pleasure.

Lost in snow. Treading muddy February roads where hikers trip and chalets grip each sharp brown peak, we suck on shiny crimson sheets of bitter berry. Bracing fun in a high dry sun.

Urban millions, stranded at the palace gate outside bright tiles that tell such tales. Wishing for wind towers to cool summer fires. No glimmer of them in halls of gleaming mirror multiplying modern heads of state.

Smiling on cue at the queen under glass. Shiny bedroom fixture among vintage TVs and old radios. Monarchs Plugged in. Tuned out. Listening for news from a vanishing life. Needing machines to change minds.

Pausing at the Shah's thinking chair to wonder
what was in his head?
what did he intend for us?

where are we now?
where is he

elegant son of his father, empty vessel filled with molten steel, shaping guns and tanks to fire off a lie so big, it cannot be denied.

A lie that freezes Sassanids and Achaemenids in matching curls and marching tunics.

A lie that lopped off the wings of women in command and in control. At Persepolis once. Museum beauties now. Relief etched on concrete walls.

In the modern art museum, revolutionary propaganda and holy writ. Angering, consoling.

Early delicate pitchers and curved thin spouts. History clear as glass. Reflecting. Shattered.

*

We enter a blue world. Tiled, painted, petalled, arched. Dark wood tables under stewing lamb, pestled into a paste of peas, parsley, lime. Tawny tea and vibrant rosewater pastries.

- It looks like my grandmother's house, says Mirza, worried I won't like this tradition.
- Things have improved because now a woman can divorce her husband if he has not paid her the housekeeping fee.

That's enlightened, I say.
- But if he has beaten her for neglecting her job she cannot divorce him.
Enthusiastically, she goes on
-I had to get permission from my husband for a passport with unlimited travel.
Her fine young man beams intelligently at me.
- Did you give it?
-With my blessing!

Pale walls and gleaming wood. Carpet curtains.
Wrought iron windows. Railings draped around eating.
-It is all they allow us to do.
So we eat and we eat. Joyfully.
Try this and this and this…

With salty watered yogurt whitening our nights, our every meal and conversation
converting us to calm acceptance, insisting we have health

Ingesting god.

*

In the hotel, hotly packing to leave. Wanting to stay.

If you have no unnecessary travel, warns the embassy…Necessary for whom? Whose need to be here? Who needs to be here?

Lured down to the lobby for good-byes. Last
conversations.

-How can we build a national theatre. Like you have
in Canada?
First comes the freedom to fail

-Such a pleasure to meet you. Poetry is my passion
too. Don't be upset for me. I am used to this prison.
I grew up with the bombs. I have lived all my life in
dark colours, not dancing

covering my hair.

**Patricia Keeney** is an award-winning author of over a dozen volumes of published poems, novels and criticism. A long-time professor of English, Creative Writing and Humanities at Toronto's York University, she has taught and given readings across Canada, the US, Europe, Asia and Africa. Her work has been translated into French, German, Spanish, Bulgarian, Hindi and Chinese. Website: wapiti words.ca

# Brenda Clews

## For Beksinski, 1929-2005

*'I consist of*
*doubts'**

In the orange sun, trove. I found.
Fe

murs, tib-tib-ia, bro

ken illi-illa-illiums, spines like
ishfish

bibsribs car-casss, humor-ouses, skulls heap

Piles.

A disintegrating burlap mesh, splintered bones hail
down
ossified cells.

Osteographies
decay.

Like Beksinski bone-writing his canvases
, ravages of knuckle metacarpals.

Innocent burnt carnelian, that.
Ground rock, carmine cochineal in
sects, dye, die blood paint.

Fossil-ate-ting tunnels
of human existence.
Crematoria, charnels ma
ssss graves. Anonymity, anon anon ymity.

Smell the dust of despair
falling from paint brushes.

His canvases stretch like a shroud
our brutal civilization.

Bright day sun rising yellow
wavefields.

---

* "Beksiński on the meaning of his art."
*'the only wisdom I wish to pass on*
*is doubt'*
https://youtu.be/1EsYHvVtb34

**Brenda Clews** is a Zimbabwe-born Canadian multimedia poet, painter, videopoet & photographer. Her books include Tidal Fury (Guernica, 2016), also in an Italian translation, Furia delle marree (PlusPlas Edizioni, 2024) and a prose poetry novella, Fugue in Green (Quattro, 2017). She's published in journals and e-zines. Her artwork has appeared on journal covers, in solo & group shows- it is also featured on her book covers. Her website is https://brendaclews.com.

# Brett Campbell

## Army Veteran

From his windowsill
he rolls another cigarette,
bars on the window and in his bloodshot eyes
in this working-class slum.

His pension pays for this room he rents
fully furnished with mice
that eat those crumbs he misses
from these cat food sandwiches.

He wakes up screaming most nights from gunfire
still ringing in his ears and the stench of corpses
he shall remember to his dying breath,
alone and forgotten on the 11th day of November.

# Trial by Fire

The victim accused,
displays scars plastic surgery
cannot hide.

Her testimony recorded:
the dent she made with a hammer,
trespassing on plant property.

The lawyer
is the best
the military can buy.

She listens and begins to believe
Nagasaki, 1945 was a crime
and she is guilty.

A judge decides
in favour of General Electric.

**Brett Campbell**'s poems have appeared in many different literary journals and anthologies including The Grammateion, Lichen, Labour of Love, Phoenix Anthology 2001, The Art Bar Poetry Series Team Reading Anthology and others. He is the author of two collections of poetry, I SEND LETTERS, published in 2004, and Alchemy, published in 2025.

# John Oughton

## FOR HAFIZ OF SHIRAZ

*(Lines from "Arise, O Cup-Bearer"*
*English translation by Gertrude Lowthian Bell)*

Where shall I rest, when the still night through.
Beyond thy gateway, oh Heart of my heart,
The bells of the camels lament and cry:
"Bind up thy burden again and depart!"

There is no peace for the exile,
the prisoner, protestor, outspoken artist, bare-headed girl.
All are launched into thrashing seas
by the cruel winds of theocracy.

Hafiz, his invisible heart welcoming wine and damsels,
yet spins his feet beyond the body
into the vortex of illumination,
nameless heaven, both sensual and transcendent.

In a Tehran museum at night, dark and still,
a sad melody arises from santur and dabdab
spirit vibrations that accompany
Hafiz's ghostly chant.

The waves run high, night is clouded with fears,
And eddying whirlpools clash and roar;
How shall my drowning voice strike their ears

Whose light-freighted vessels have reached the shore?

**John Oughton** grew up in Guelph, Ontario. After sojourns in Nova Scotia, Iraq, Egypt, and Japan, he now resides in Toronto's Beaches area. He has published six poetry books (Most recently The Universe and All That), a mystery novel, and a book about post-secondary teaching as well as around 500 articles, reviews, blogs, and interviews and several chapbooks (most recently, Double Vision). John retired as Professor of Learning and Teaching from Centennial College, where he taught English and then led faculty development. His current pursuits include guitar, photography, and kayaking. He is the Treasurer e of the Writers Union of Canada.

# Peter Taylor

## Cities Within Us

*The cross and orb that top the Dresden Frauenkirche were even crafted by a British goldsmith whose father took part in the fire raids in February 1945.*

*BBC NEWS*

Built for a baroque Emperor in his Florence on the Elbe,
the Dresden Frauenkirche stands serenely against a lasting sky
in Canaletto's painting: her graceful dome,
the Stone Bell, hard as Meissen porcelain,
deflecting the impotent cannon balls of invading princes
to rise above a busy marketplace, calling
her faithful to the catechisms of Luther
and eternal anthem of the Ode to Joy.

But when they came for her on Ash Wednesday,
unrepentant winged furies dropping
4,000-pound blockbuster bombs with incendiaries
to create das Höllenfeuer,
there was no water for the hoses
or shelters for the people,
only flames and whirlwind and terror.

The dead not cremated in their own homes

were stacked in funeral pyres in the streets
and torched with flamethrowers.

She alone withstood the bombing and the fire
to become a sacred kiln heated above 1000° Celsius,
annealing her faithful to bone ash and eternity,
until dawn's despair awoke her ecstasy
and she collapsed onto
the altar's final sermon in stone.

Her spire cross, twisted into a bombsight,
lay hidden beneath the ruins
for half a century.

Until a new cross, forged in steel
and burnished with gilt by the son of her enemy,
resurrects her random stones to bring
hope and reconciliation to a city
drowned by fire and risen
from the ashes of its mortal clay.

How many died? Who knows the answer?
a great stone asks in silence.

The answer lies within us.
The cities lie within us.

**Peter Taylor** has published seven books and chapbooks and his poems have appeared in journals and anthologies in Canada and in more than a dozen countries. His latest book, Cities Within Us (Guernica Editions), was shortlisted for the Welsh

Poetry Book Awards, and Antietam (Winning Writers), his experimental verse play on the Civil War, was awarded honourable mention in the War Poetry Contest in Northampton, Massachusetts. He holds a master's degree in English Literature and has worked as a printer and bookbinder, medical publisher, institute director and non-profit executive. Born in Edmonton, he lives in Aurora.

# Josephine LoRe

## A Single Leaf

this poem is a leaf
falling from a tree

this poem is the stillness
after the last echo sounds

the pause between an exhalation
and the next inhale

this poem is gravel
embedded into knee

an offering of thanks
for a crust of week-old bread

this poem is the rumble
of armoured trucks
a deluge of debris

this poem is every story
every footfall walking
further from belongings
step by step toward the safety
beyond borders

this poem is a pacifier
in the dead grasses
by the roadside

family photos
curling in the flame

this poem is fingers
playing a white piano
for the very last time

a baker in a land of foreign tongue
braiding dough

this poem is centuries of steady leaving

flaxen-haired children
playing in the grasses
of the Canadian West
hearing tales of their babusya

this poem is the pattern
finely painted on a paschal egg

a ribbon woven
a dance steeped in folklore

this poem is empty words and hollow lies

this poem is arrogance
the hubris of ambition
a heart of anthracite

this poem is despotic
the colour of blue sky
golden sun

a tattered flag at dusk

this poem is the world watching
too afraid to condemn

the pause between an inhalation
and the last exhale

this poem is the silence that thunders
after the last echo

this poem, a single leaf
falling from a tree

this poem is a doll, trampled
a fountain, withered
markings for growth pencilled on a door jam
of a house in which the roof
has fallen in

this poem is a whimper in the night

this poem is Syria,
Passchendaele, Dakar
this poem is Dresden, Tripoli
Ukraine

this poem is polished leather
marching in the mud
to the counterpoint of hatred

this poem is a drone

the barrel of a gun

this poem is a daffodil
sprung from ground
no-one there to marvel

this poem is a prayer
unanswered in the dark

a graveyard
headstones tumbled in the tumult

this poem is hope
navigating in a blind sky

this poem is fear
the stench of death

a seed swallowed
in the belly of the plenty

this poem is numb

this poem is sirens, air raids, blackouts
a mother shushing a wailing child
eyes dimmed
by the hunger and the horror

this poem is robin muted
barn owl stunned into silence

this poem is humanitarian
drop by single drop

the cold press of metal

this poem is making its way over rubble
the body yearning for comfort
for respite, for home

this poem is the blue glow
of late-night news
the drone, the drone

this poem is Gallipoli
the battle of Batoche, Beirut
Leningrad, Michilimackinac, Kyiv

this poem is a weightless child
borne on weary shoulders

the elderly, infirm left behind

this poem is the same mistake
repeated

power, greed, and lust
all the venial sins
and all the mortal sins combined
and circles
circles upon circles of inner hell

this poem is the atrocities of man
barriers, fences, roadblocks
undiluted hate

this poem is a cry tearing the veil of night

this poem is a leaf
a single leaf falling from a single tree

this poem is a stream running red
bodies rotting into ground

this poem is letters undelivered
lovers lost to each other in forever
babies not conceived and never born

this poem is fields untilled, unsown
song unsung
country churches
windows smashed and broken

this poem is chickens left to rummage
cows unmilked, sheep unshorn
a horse dying of starvation
on cold ground

this poem is the moon
hung low in desperation
the deportation of Acadians
at the point of bayonet
Tibet

Jerusalem, Berlin:  walls of wailing
walls of brick

the floating exodus of Viet Nam
this poem is Mogadishu, Rwanda
the Lost Boys of Sudan

this poem is drownings in the harbour
the Noche Triste, the Fourth Reich

this poem is the West Bank and the Nile
the War of 1812, the war of secession
the war against repression
the war against concession

this poem is a reed basket
Daniel and the lion
Samson shorn
this poem is David
without a slingshot or a stone

this poem is a leaf, a single leaf

falling from a tree
a single tree
floating on a river

a river turning red

*"A Single Leaf" was published by WordCity, https://wordcitylit.ca/2024/10/11/a-single-leaf-a-poem-by-josephine-lore/*

**Josephine LoRe**'s poetry has been read on stage and in global zoom-rooms, put to music, danced, integrated into visual art, and published in anthologies and collections in 11 countries and 4 languages. Publications include FreeFall and Vallum in Canada, Fixed & Free and Tiny Seed Journal in the US, Constellate in England, Ireland's Same Page Anthology, and the Wild Word in Germany. Josephine has two collections, Unity and the Calgary Herald Bestseller The Cowichan Series. https://www.josephinelorepoet.com/

# I.B. Iskov

## Rumour Has It

I pour over the print,
digest nauseating news.
These terrorist days,
every staggering story proves volatile.

Rumour has it I work inside a cubicle,
concealed under wraps
alongside history books
with compatible companions
sticking to their cell phones.

We discover the repetition
at our feet – Hitler and Khamenei
with equal disgust.

Moving from the grey matter
of fact to a bomb shelter
on the lakefront covered with black cloth
keeps me from staying home,
but this is no dry run.

I return at moonrise
and wash up on a sheltered shore.

My collaborators believe I hold the pencil
like a knife,
but they only whisper the reality:
Any woman apologizing on her knees

is never at a loss for words
and should be held responsible
for the gossip.

It is my custom to wrestle with injustice,
set myself on a mad course
to organize nouns and verbs
and egg shells,
maybe even broken glass.

I don't fantasize a happy solution.
Jews and dogs and good Christian children
are all susceptible to the same fate.
Brute creation demands this.
Ask any executioner holding a gun.

**I.B. (Bunny) Iskov** – is the Founder of The Ontario Poetry Society, www.theontariopoetrysociety.ca. Bunny has several poetry collections, and she has won numerous contest prizes. Bunny is the recipient of the Absolutely Fabulous Woman Award, 2017. Her most recent collection is "One Place the Light Remains", Mosaic Press, 2025.

# Lynn Xu

## Let the Memory Live — for Jun. 4, 1989

*Jun. 4th each year always reminds me of what happened on the Tiananmen Square in 1989 that has changed track of my life forever.*

How much does it take to forget
yet how little will it take to remember -
that stormy night
courage flooded the city
in poppy red

when the wind calms down
the world becomes a mirror
the living becomes a shadow
and the shadow comes alive
through memories

Let the memory live!

# Poppies

1.
Poppies unfold their petals
like banners unfurling passion
like flames flaring with courage
when crushed, they drop
petal by petal
like blood spilling
and their seeds buried deep
so each year they come back
to remind us of the passion and courage
as the blood-red petals unfold

2.
Each year early June
the passion of poppies
burns through each petal
shouting: we remember!
their bright colour remembers
the blood lost and
the hearts still bleeding
their black seeds
like eyes
piercing through darkness
they remember
no matter how much time passed
no matter oceans across

# Today It Rained

The kind of rain that extinguishes fire
fire in so many hearts

the kind of rain that washes away stains
stains from so much blood

the kind of rain that sprouts buds
buds that bloom memories of a time

After so many years on this day
it rained

# As A Poet

Forgive me for seeking only
to see the light
for ignoring all the dark corners
that are always there
because I came
all the way
from darkness
to live this life
only once

**Lynn Xu**, an observer, a reader, a learner of life, it is my strong belief that though we cannot choose the culture we are born to, we can break all boundaries by expanding our inner visions, and poetry is one of the doors that opens my vision.

# Hiram Larew

## You or Me

We all need to realize
that most people worldwide
pick their teeth --
Nearly everyone does
everywhere

And if that seems too odd a way
to leave war alone
Then someone should maybe point out
that each of us
everyone young or old
in our own way
Sits down at the day's end
to watch birds head home.

*This poem first appeared in Larew's collection, Patchy Ways (CyberWit, 2023).*

# Given Over

Just once
and in the spirit of whatever winks
please help me create a dearly different religion
Steeped in hoot toot
and with whistling almighties waving at me

A worship of the given over unto
and believed in
as heavens come upon us
from the get go

Yes teach me how to pray like vines growing up porches
or to sing out as proudly as jokes do
or to greet everyone eagerly
like I'm dashing past holy

And with what's twisted in knots
Let it be so
as undone and ever shall be
by the faith of my sillies

Yes let me become cartwheeling trumpets
or those abracadabra blessings
from visions of whatsoever
all juicy laden with stings and say so

And so on and unto
into the rolling hereafters

for once only
to such great beyonds
on devout soap bubble amens

*This poem first appeared in Hidden Peaks.*

# Say Damn

Wet towels are who?
Nuts went where?
Toe nails got what?

In a roundabout way
I'm asking you to shut up
And vote.

And I don't care at all
About what squirts
Or how Auntie Boo lied
Or why creeks piss.

Because if there's one thing
I know besides my bladder
It's history and how pitiful stupid
Re-telling it can be.

So do as I say and dammit
X that box
Extra good like I am
Then yes go chew on some dimes
If you want to.

*This poem first appeared in The Skinny Poetry Journal.*

**Hiram Larew**'s work appears widely in English and other languages. His most recent collection, This Much Very, was published in 2025 by Alien Buddha

Press. He founded Poetry X Hunger to bring a world of poets to the anti-hunger cause. HiramLarewPoetry.com and PoetryXHunger.com

# Sylvia Petter

## Sticks and Stones

"Sticks and stones may break my bones, but words will never hurt me." I sang this at school when nasty things were being said about me. Self-preservation of sorts. I needed to cope in an environment where unequal arms were the rule.

Today, I see how words can be dangerous, and so are reviled by those in power for they can slip through everywhere and combine in a force of rhythm that in its cadence can overpower. Why else do those in power want to shut them down on the internet, in songs, in poems?

Words are power. They cannot be grasped and shot. They live on to fertilise thinking, uphold truth and shine light where it can have an influence. They are stronger than bullets, sticks and stones. For they are hope.

**Sylvia Petter**, born 1949 in Vienna, is an Australian. Her stories have been widely published. Her debut novel, All the Beautiful Liars, was published by Eye Books, UK, in 2021. She has a PhD in Creative Writing from the University of New South Wales in Sydney, and is currently working on her second novel, Ambergris.

# Claudia Piccinno

## Missiles over Tehran

*This poem is about innocent passengers and crew of Flight PS 752 perished by the missiles of Iranian regime.*

The future crashes with the plane,
dreams die after takeoff.
A delirium of missiles over Tehran,
war runs wild—
this is no video game.
We touch the abyss of humankind.
The dog and cat upon a couch
remind us of distant love.
You ask me what remains after a bomb?
Imagine a field without flowers,
an orchestra without instruments,
a choir without voices,
an ocean drained of water.
Only craters of waste,
smoke, desolation—
nothing left to recycle,
a species to reset,
no chromosome left for reproduction.

# NERINA

*This poem is about Italian women who helped partisans and fought with them in order to free their country from German soldiers during 2nd World War)*

Nerina rode her bike,
pretending to be in a little hurry.
The shots touched her saddle,
her heart creaked in the trash.
She swallowed messages
and ink many times
in order that the words
were not extracted from her.
She did not like to remember
her fear while running in the barn,
the adrenaline of dissent
shone in her eyes
and euphoria of the revolution
was swinging.
This epitaph Nerina wanted-
I did not do anything special
the strength of emancipation
must be our habitual courage.

**Author's Note:**
I wish to express my solidarity with Iranian women and the country's new generations, slaughtered or driven to exhaustion by the lack of freedom and desperation over the economic and political crisis that their country is experiencing. I believe that beyond international political lines, every self-respecting intellectual must lend his own voice to the service of civilians forced into silence and deprived of all rights. Resistance does not require grand proclamations but concrete examples like those who have unfortunately been harshly repressed. It is our task to carry forward the voices of the most vulnerable.

**Claudia Piccinno**

**Claudia Piccinno** is a teacher, poet and translator. She has been the Continental Director for Europe in the World Festival Poetry from April 2019 to september 2021, she is the artistic director for the Versatili Versi and Con-versi-amo con il Mondo festivals. She is the recipient of many national awards among these: Gold medal Frate Ilaro 2017, Ossi di Seppia prize 2020, Pannunzio 2022, Murazzi aknowledgement for culture, translation prizes in Paestum, Massa Carrara, Mugello. She is meritorious of the Municipality of Castel Maggiore (Bo) for cultural merits.

# Emil Nicolae

## THE POEM AS A PET

The park in the city center
watched over through the years
now by a saint now by a general now by a
schoolteacher
placed one after another on the same pedestal—
today it is the place where ladies and gentlemen
walk their dogs and cats
monkeys and poets
(Ferdousi Khayyam Saadi Hafez)
to the cadence of the funeral march
performed by the municipal brass band

each day you are forced to slip through there
with a hesitant step trying
to keep your balance by holding tight
to the leash of the poem's first line—
"April is the cruellest month." (*)

---

(*) acc. T. S. Eliot, The Waste Land, 1922;

# THE COBALT VASE

And the lilac has bloomed again lilac-purple
beside the concrete coffin
into which your childhood home has vanished
and again you crouch there
beneath the lilac scent
watching the girl's movements
with her sturdy bust
and again you see her bring the cobalt vase
with Persian patterns
and place it on the balustrade

then lean forward
to shake out the striped blanket
and again you tremble with emotion
when her mountain woman's breast
draws near the cobalt vase
which topples over and shatters
with a lilac sound

# ALMOST A FABLE

*All the characters in history*
*are silent*

deities emperors religious masters
geniuses of science and art philosophers
political leaders heroes criminals
friends and enemies – without order
proclamations warnings promises –
only images submerged in the past

today's noises are only
our words about them

# THE SCALP

It is so cold this autumn
that the apple ritualistically peeled
in a shop window in Tehran
slowly meticulously
with a silver knife
and then looked at in the light
of the sun with teeth
resembles a child's head
that has been scalped

# OMNIA VINCIT AMOR

She sits down beside you and whispers
“love means being close”
(even though some proclaim the opposite)
and you decide to experiment
focusing your gaze on
one square centimeter of freckles
on her shoulder (a delicate perspective) or
on her breast (an erotic perspective) or
on her thigh (an intimate perspective)
until it becomes a garden from Brobdingnag (*)

---

(*) the “land of giants” in A Voyage to Brobdingnag (t. 2 of the cycle Travels into Several Remote Nations of the World by Jonathan Swift, any edition)

**Author’s Note:**
**POETRY AND FREEDOM**

Here is a confession: when I began to write, in my adolescence (during the communist dictatorship!), I chose poetry because it seemed to me to be the literary genre that offers the fullest sense of freedom. Of course, I arrived at this idea intuitively, but also as a result of my regular readings, among which the great authors of classical Persian culture (translated into Romanian) were not absent. That is why I was surprised and saddened to see that a people who had, in its deepest fiber, the vocation of freedom could be shackled and mistreated by dictatorship (and it is not the only case in human history).

Poetry arrested? Poetry manipulated? Poetry used ideologically? In other words, life in general — for there is no poetry without life and no life without poetry… That is why I support the liberation movement of the Iranian people, with the hope that it will rediscover the true values that established it within universality.

**EMIL NICOLAE** (Emanuel Nadler, b. 1947 at Bacau, Romania; he lives in Piatra Neamț) – writer, journalist, museum curator, art critic, translator. Member of the Writers' Union of Romania (since 1990).
He has published 29 books of poetry, essays, studies, and art albums. His most recent publication is Emanuel Speaks (poetry & confessions, 2022).
He has received poetry and literary criticism awards granted by the Writers' Union – Iași Branch (2000, 2006, 2012, 2018, 2023), as well as the Order of Cultural Merit, Knight rank, awarded by the President of Romania (2004).
He holds the title of "Honorary Citizen of the Municipality of Piatra-Neamț" (2018).

# Josie Di Sciascio-Andrews

## The Chestnut Tree

He was an individual.

His beauty,
Asserting his heart-
Shaped leaves
Against the sky
made everyone's day.

A neighbour.
A benevolent friend
Blossoming anew
Each spring.

His flowers: words
That spoke of life,
Of freedom to exist.

Then lightning hit
And soggy with rain,
His heaviest branch
Tore part of his trunk.

For weeks, like a stroke
Victim, the useless limb
Lay lifeless on the grass
While he continued
To thrive and bloom.

The owner

In charge of the property
Wanted order.
Abhorred this mess.

The injured tree
No longer fit
His paradigm
Of what a tree should be,
Though he could have
Been trimmed
And saved.

Soon the tree cutters
Arrived to behead it.
A shorn torso was left.

A profusion of tendrils
Emerged like human hands
Waving sos messages.

Obsessed with order,
The owner redoubled
His efforts. Had it razed
To the ground.

Soon, one branch
Like an arm, shot
Out of the circular base.
Heart shaped leaves
A clear message.

In uniforms, the tree authorities
Came to dig out the roots.

To eliminate the idea of him.
Filled in the grave with soil.
Covered it with grass.

In my mind
The tree still lives.
It greets me where it stood
As I drive or walk by.

His words of life
Still bloom
In books of poems
He wrote in white and green.
So too, that owner's heartless
Prose forever stings.

I would rather be that tree
Than one who is blind
To life and beauty

I wrote this poem "**The Chestnut Tree**" in February 2026 to express my solidarity with the innocent people of Iran, who are being oppressed and brutally killed by the authorities for peacefully protesting for their human rights. Everyone who is born deserves to live a life of peace and freedom to manifest their goals and dreams along with their families and friends. Any autocratic system that oppresses human life and environmental preservation is a system against life and hence a system of death and destruction.

I pray that the words we write as poets and as lovers of life will breathe a spirit of renewal and justice in the hearts and minds of leaders who may have power to put an end to the violent oppression of the innocent and beautiful young people of Iran. They deserve a chance to live a normal life and to actualize their beautiful futures in peace.

**Josie Di Sciascio-Andrews**

# Mosque

We escaped into the sweltering darkness of an alley.
Footsteps of armed soldiers echoed on the
humid cobblestones, feverishly reflecting the
illumination of the mosque beyond the rooftops.
The light led us to the monolith. From mullioned
windows, telescopes scanned the city. High
tech devices with weapon capabilities. We hid from
their beams into a shadowed stairway down
to the riverbank. In the twilight, we witnessed
people being carried off by the current; children
waving their arms, drowning. And an old oracle
slumped by the edge, watching. *It happens*
*everyday now.* He cried dolefully. *It's the end of*
*times.*

**Josie Di Sciascio-Andrews** has written seven collections of poetry and two non-fiction books. Her work appears in various journals and anthologies among which: Canadian Literature, The Malahat Review, Descant, The Canada Literary Review, Acta Victoriana, Canadian Poetry Review, The Blue Nib and Lothlorien, among others. Her poetry won first prize in the 2023 International Poetry Prize in Rome's Antonio De Ferraris contest. Her poem "The First Time I Heard Leonard Cohen" was nominated for the 2022 Pushcart Prize. Her latest book of poems, A Nomenclature for Light was released September 2025 by Mosaic Press. Josie is a member of The League of Canadian Poets, the Ontario Poetry Society, the Italian Canadian Writers Association and

The Heliconian Club for Women in the Literary Arts. She teaches workshops for Poetry in Voice and is the host & coordinator of The Oakville Literary Cafe series.

# Elizabeth Barnes

## Black on Black

Most recently
It has come to light
That five cops in Memphis
Wearing body cams
No less
On a traffic stop
Beat
Black on
Black
The innocent man
To his
Death
while
Taking on the
mindset
Of their
oppressors
And
Meting out their
own
Twisted sense of
Justice
And for what?
Their own rage
And help
less
ness
Against their
own
People

And their
Lot
To have been
Born
Black
In a white
man's
World.

# Refusal

We the non-compliant
we who choose to be left to our own devices
we who choose
we who fill up the streets with slang and subversion
bouncing basketballs
loud impenetrable music
we who bring down the value of your real estate

We who refuse:
you fear our insolence
you fear our bodies
you fear our raw untethered energy--
we who refuse to work your work

Poetry and writing poetry have helped me along the way, to understand myself and others and to make sense of the comings and goings of this world. It has opened my eyes to many layers of experience and meaning which I will continue to explore. **Elizabeth Barnes**

# Elana Wolff

## A Pure Anticipation

We couldn't wait,
we waited. We feared
to act,
we acted. Action was required

and a pure anticipation.
Voices in the millions risen,
wakened to a knowing/feeling
consciousness

accessible across translations: all.

We're fed by the momentum
and unwilling
to relent,
but are we able
to prevail
against the weapons of the state?

Say promise
Say there's rightfulness
Say agency
Say urgency
Say sky is listening, nigh
Say earthly light
Say Saint, say Saint Anaphora and say it like a
mantra
Say Apostrophe, Apostrophe

Say wind, say whipping wind
Say what can't be said enough of now

## We felt like wearing orange sports caps

cycling up the mountainside,
riding in our bright
green cotton shirts.
We visioned being carried—
light as autumn seed pods,
wheeling our legs like whirled batons,
flinging our caps
behind us—      to the wind.
You on the rackety handlebars; I on the rickety seat.

We passed the place that burned to earth;
thousands gathered, ranting, chanting. Fervently,

we kept on cycling, you and I—
two women, pledged to freedom.
                                        Up the mountain,
resolute—
riding on our rightfulness, our colours,
                                                    &
momentum.

*previously published in Woman, Life, Freedoms: Poems for the Iranian Revolution, Guernica Editions, 2025*

**Elana Wolff** writes from the ancestral land of the Haudenosaunee and Huron-Wendat First Nations in Ontario. Her poems have recently been featured in Anacapa Review, Best Canadian Poetry 2024, Blood+Honey, Gyroscope Review, Horseshoe

Literary Journal, The Nelligan Review, Paragon Magazine, Pinhole Poetry, Public Reverie, and The/tEmz /Review. Her cross-genre Kafka-quest work, Faithfully Seeking Franz, received the 2024 Canadian Jewish Literary Award in the category of Jewish Thought and Culture. Her poetry collection, Everybody Knows a Ghost, is soon forthcoming.

# Mahdi Ganjavi

## Iran

Oh Iran,
to know you,
I need you to be free.
Knowing the bird in the cage
is knowledge of the cage.
I have known you all my life
as far as your wings
bent and scarred -
have reached the bar.
As far as your neck is made to turn down
resulting in your head
looking at the ground.
Knowing you
has been
knowing the form of your confinement.
Knowing myself in you
has been
recognition of desire
in times of trouble.
Iran,
I wish to know you
and for that
you need to be free.
Seeing the steps you take forward
before flying,
seeing the turning of the rain
on your feathers
when your eyes

do not hide
the restlessness of a longing.
Oh Iran,
knowing anyone
is knowing them
at the moment of their freedom.

# Freedom is an Iranian garden

Freedom
is an Iranian garden—
not loose,
not wild,
but made,
with calculation
and patience.

A garden
designed for walking,
with fountains
that have seen the world
through the eyes of water—

water
that did not fall from the sky,
but rose from underground,
from the qanat,
from the soil's collective memory.

Freedom
is a flow,
not a command.
It arrives
if the path
has not been sealed with concrete.

The garden gate—
the main axis—
is straight,
not for speed,

but for visibility,
so that the body
knows

where it stands.
In the chahar-bagh,
people have the right
to walk straight
or to turn;
they have the right
to change their route
in the moment.

No camera
turns movement
into suspicion.

The trees
are old—
older than governments,
older than states of emergency.

Roots
do not appear in reports,
yet
everything
stands on them.

Shade
is the right to sit,
the right to be silent,
the right to have privacy.

Around the garden
there is a wall—
not for confinement,
but so that
freedom
can be recognized
from the desert.

The wall
is the boundary of the garden,
not the boundary of the human.

The pavilion
stands at the center of the garden,
not above it;
power,
if it exists,
is visible,
questionable
from all sides.

The flowerbeds
are not identical.
No tree
is pruned
for being different.
Diversity
is not a threat;
it is design.

Freedom is that garden
which,
if its water is cut off,

still—
the roots
know
how,
in the deepest
soils of yesterday,
to build the future.

# Today

Today
I learned that I am a rioter.
Yesterday I was only a protester,
but overnight,
on the 20:30 news,
I was promoted.

Today
they told me I am an infiltrator—
interesting,
since I still
lose my own house key,
though I have no escape
from infiltrating poverty.

Today
to my list of names
they added *Zionist mercenary*,
even though
of geography
all I know
is the line for ever-more expensive necessities.

Today
I became ISIS—
a multi-level promotion,
with these same hands
that cannot even
lift a clod of earth.

Today

the judge said:
"This individual is *corrupt on earth*."
I looked at the earth
and saw
no corruption—
only my foot
tied to a metal chair.

Today, at once,
I became an enemy of God
and *irreligious*:
I have a sword
and no faith—
remarkable progress in a single day.

Today
they called me
a separatist,
while my only wish
is that
I myself
not be torn apart.

Today I became
a seditionist,
a regime-toppler,
a foreign agent,
a mercenary—
with a salary
whose deposit receipts
are still being prepared.

Today

I realized
I am no longer a person.
I am a file,
with a red cover
and many names.

Today
my names
are more than myself,
and tomorrow
surely
a new name
will be added to me.

Tomorrow,
if my voice is not heard,
do not say I fell silent.
Say:
the case
was closed.

# Your grave will be washed

*Remembering Baktash and Manouchehr Neyestani*

Your grave will be washed.
The graves of all Iranian writers will be washed.
The scared, broken, and kicked 'pen and what they inscribe'
will return to the throat.
The joy of every mourner
will come out of the blood.
The soil will return its trust.
The unmarked corpse
will no longer be thirsty.
The exile
will return home
in the arms of dead readers.
Even if you have been dead for years,
that chain that has to this day cuffed you to the hospital bed;
will open.
The grave of all the languages of Iran will be washed.
Dead languages
will reveal again
the secret in each other's ears.
Books that were never written
will return
to the absent shelves.
Pieces of each tomb
that they have broken
will rejoin each other.
Pieces of each grave
that they will break.

Poems
will be written
with the words that have returned
from their ultimate demise.

**Mahdi Ganjavi** is a poet, publisher, and professor at the University of Toronto's Faculty of Information. His work explores Middle Eastern studies, Cold War knowledge production, and print culture. He is the author of Education and the Cultural Cold War: The Franklin Book Program in Iran (I.B. Tauris). As editor-in-chief of Asemana Magazine and director of Asemana Books, he amplifies diasporic, underrepresented, progressive, and decolonial voices. Ganjavi has published a novel, two short story collections, and five poetry collections, including The Galaxy Has No Memory of Sunset. His work bridges scholarship, resistance, and cultural memory through multilingual, community-driven publishing.

# Mbizo Chirasha

## CASAVA REPUBLICS

*Juba*

Child of lost sperm in sunsets of
political masturbation

*Wagadugu*

Deadline of our revolutions

*Darfur*

Constipated stomach ,disease ravaged,
bloodless dozing  monk.

*Nairobi*

Culture lost in the dust of Saxon lexicon
and gutter slang

*Soweto*

Xenophobia Drunk and Afro-phobia sloshed.

*Marikana*

Cervical blister of the unfinished
revolution fungi.

*Harare*

Corruption polonium deforming elders into
political hoodlums

*Congo*

Lodge of secessionists and human
guillotines

# SAD REVOLUTIONARY LULLABIES

……..Sing songs of afghan circumcised,

Damascus masturbating bullets

Sing *Belafonte* Sing!

Of revolutions that never crawled, sing!

*Lumumba*, see whiz kids castrating
political gods

*Nkurumah,* see them mutilating
revolutionary goddesses

Sing *Kunta*, Sing *Kinte*

I am tired of revolutions importing
colonial mood,

Propaganda decayed pimps frying anthems
like *frikadels*

Tired savages roasting constitutions in
corruption oil pans

Sing songs of freedoms that never walked,
Sing!

# RHETORICS

*Mandela,* the summer sun that rose through
rubbles of our winter

Gadafi and Sadamu making *shadufs* and
pyramids

……. another spring

*Obama and Osama* pulling rich political
carrot in *Segorong*

Robin Island slept golden nightmares and
charcoal dreams,

Soweto virgins cracking their under feet
in the long walk to freedom

Faces carrying the burden of freedom and
anthems.

## The Road To Zvegona

Is fading the memory of its son,
Who for words must ride the night
Fleeing ears that hear thunder on a baby's purity guggle,
Zvegona, my homestead,
Ancestors are watching
Elders on a scheming mission
Trading lies with more lies
The road to Zvegona
Your Sideroads sigh
Your song is silent
Only hiccups of mothers greet the sun
Yearning for the return of the bearded child
Who lives on the strings of truth
Truth refused a seat at the council of baboons on the lagoons
Goons settling scores on the assumptions that a boy has a price,
Well, the boy true has a price
But not one you can pay with looted coins
The boy has shaved his hair not his brains
The boy has slipped his boots on and truth has raised its flag
And the spirits of truth sing his Achilles heels on,
So Zvegona, the village of the lucky poet,
Grow thistles and thorns
Feed cattle and goats
The boy has shaved his beard
Ready for a walk back, to shave the land of all pretentious shenanigans
Uprooting the weeds and weevils

Repair the kraal too,
Where roosters shall announce light unto the land,
Currently bent double under the gargantuan weight of lying tongues.
Zvegona, you are my yesterday
Zvegona, you are my tomorrow in whatever form, shape or .......

## Between Steps

Ancestral fire, flames licking the dreams,
Of a knee, low in raised silence,
A sunny bud, brooding on black soils,
Am the kite, whose string is loosed from the root,
Flying, prying, praying,
I step between steps like a dancer,
But far from it for am a panther,
Black like midnight on an empty sky,
The stars speak to my soul in whispered hopes,
Dressing the wounds my father planted on my tongue,
Am the small prophet with a big Horn,
Blaring a child's observed truth,
I cry not for milk but for water,
Kindness is offered by a nameless priest,
Whose motivation lay in the cradle of ancient texts,
Reminding the living to tread with care,
For wings have flown riches to a beggar and poverty to the king,
Am presently at nowhere,
Waiting to go somewhere,

Unsure of something,
Trusting no one but the milky way,
Where science studies gods and the mystics of earthlings,
Am the stairs staring at dusk with hopes of dawn,
Am in most dreams where miracles push disbelief to the edge,
And while here, I sing words that to many,
Sound like a fairy tale from Aesop's stable,
For to lean too hard on the missing part,
Is to follow the dictates of naysayers,
Who know the end of all they hate with a common curse in tow,
Which resilience does deny the ear of one still baring his soul to sunrise,
From where truth rises and rests not,
Till it says it's piece at the council of right without shades.

**Mbizo Chirasha** is the founder of the Writing Ukraine Prize and a UNESCO-RILA Affiliate Artist. He has been a Free-Speech Fellow to PEN-Zentrum Deutschland, African Fellow at IHRAF (USA), and Guest Writer at Glasgow University. His residencies include Fictional Cafe (USA), Sotambe Film Festival (Zambia), and ICACD (Ghana). He curated the *Voices of Africa* and co-edited *The Second Name of Earth is Peace*. Chirasha is chief editor at *Time of the Poet Republic*, founding editor at *WomaWords Literary Press*, and curator of *Africa Writers Caravan*. His books include *A Letter to the*

*President*, *Pilgrims of Zame*, and co-authored *Whispering Woes of Ganges and Zambezi*. His works—poetry, essays, fiction—appear in over 1000 publications worldwide, including *The Evergreen Review*, *Poetry London*, *FemAsia Magazine*, *Ink Sweat and Tears*, *The Bezine*, *Poetry Pacific*, and *Festival de Poesia Medellin*.

Facebook Account www.facebook.com/mbizowachirasha

Wikipedia www.wikipedia.com/mbizochirasha

# Niels Hav

## FREEDOM

**F**alse pride collapses sooner or later.
**R**eality seems in its structure to be governed by reason.
**E**ven despots and empires grind to an end; not
**E**ither murderers or violent political systems
**D**o last forever; then the regime falls apart.
**O**nly invincible power is the zest which every
**M**orning lifts us all out of sleep with joy and hope.

*An acrostic poem with the message: FREEDOM.*

# A FATAL DEFECT

It's a fatal defect of the human imagination
that we can't empathize with the disasters of others.
We were granted this shortcoming for our psychic
survival,
not for making blunted jokes about other people's
catastrophes. Humour is a kind of self-defence
but ironic smirking is out of order
when the tanks come rolling in and flesh and blood
from human creatures drip from the trees.

Some claim that we' haven't the right to talk about
these things without being there ourselves
without having stood there with a torn off arm
or a smashed brain in our hands.
We already wallow in terror and cynical
pornography.
Resignation is a possibility.
But we've no right either to neglect
the world's evil just because we ourselves
by some fluke landed in the whitefat ghetto.

We are eight billion people on this planet;
each one equipped with a unique individuality,
which deserve respect. Alone through simple
wisdom,
or the physical memory of our own thin skin, we
ought
to let ourselves be touched by the misfortunes of
others.
Irony is an impossible escape on the day when we
ourselves

are lying screaming in pain on the street or in a
hospital
and all internal defenses fall apart. Then it's for real.

*Translated by Per Brask*

# Arguments

Can the world be improved? First we'll have to
change
human nature. There's cause for pessimism.
Evil triumphs, and hate appears dressed up
in religion, or in the latest political uniform.

But it is more difficult yet to give up on the idea
and to resign oneself to the world as it is.
So we had to let go of the dream that our
descendants
will meet a happier future. Our genetic inheritance.

Yet none of us can imagine killing off our children's
expectations, even if we are ashamed of our own
confusion and ignorance. Joy is such a frail
material, and physical happiness is no crime.

Admitted; I'm groping in the dark. There's a
shortage
of words with real validity. Concrete suggestions
or a solid sentence with a foothold.
I cannot offer firm arguments.

But I'm affiliated with the naïve who mosey on
and want the impossible.

*Translated by Brask & Friesen*

## The Poem

Don't you put the poem
in a headlock – You are under arrest!

The poem won't obey orders.

The poem doesn't do well in isolation cells.
The poem rambles around the suburbs
rummages through other people's trash
it packs a gun.

The poem distrusts the law and the courts,
yet trusts in a higher justice.
The poem gets into arguments with any old passers-
by
barges in on the CEO
making wild accusations. Shows
no respect. Smells badly
(shit & roses).

The poem happily waits in line for a thunderstorm.
The poem spends the night in solitude
and wild ecstasy.
The poem hangs around in airports
and on board overcrowded ferries.
The poem is largely political, but hates
politics.
The poem is cantankerous,
but speaks only on rare occasions.

The poem spoils the party.
The poem is ready to take of its jacket

and meet you outside.
The poem's got a
case of the jitters.

*Translated by Heather Spears*

**Niels Hav** is a full-time writer with awards from the Danish Arts Counsil. His books are widely translated, and he is frequently interviewed by the media, as he has travelled widely in Europe, Asia, Africa, North and South America.
Niels Hav was raised on a farm in western Denmark, today he resides in the most colourful and multi-ethnic part of the Danish capital, Copenhagen.
His recent book ***Moments of Happiness*** is published by Anvil Press in Vancouver.

"...one of Denmark's most talented living poets..."
Frank
Hugus, *The Literary Review*

# Richard Harrison

## Iran Under Theocracy

A woman tells me she feared
 the morality police more
than the ordinary men who groped her flesh
 through the veil she wore every day of her
life there,
her piety nothing to them compared to her body.

But her body was nothing to the state, and that was
worse,
 for where is the escape
when the refuge has become a dungeon,
 and the holy rituals are all under
surveillance?

There is no escaping
 the strange temptations of faith.
Love is power, but power can be cruel,
 and your religion can make you forget
that though you profess to love God,
 and in God all things are possible, still,

you are measured on Earth and in Heaven
 by the way you touch the helpless in His
name.

**Richard Harrison** is the author of seven books of poetry, among them the Governor General's Award winning On Not Losing My Father's Ashes in the Flood. His work also appears in Beau Beausoleil and Deema Shehabi's anthology, Al Mutanabbi Street Starts Here: Poets and Writers Respond to the March 5, 2007 Bombing of Baghdad's 'Street of Booksellers'" and in the international photography and text exhibit about missing and executed Iraqi academics, Shadows and Light. With accompanying translation, the poem "Iran Under Theocracy" was aired first on the Farsi-language radio program Namaashoum.

# EVA Petropoulou Lianou

## Women.

I was wondering if I am free?

Do u feel free?

Nooo

Every day I walk in a street of possibilities and opportunities..

But nobody look at me

As i am a woman..

It is unspeakable how much a woman is used..

From day one

A woman needed to educate the child

To cook for a child

To learn him how to think.. Speak..

Act..

A lot for a woman to do

But what happens after..

A woman need

A woman wish

A woman word

Inexistant person

Until one day

U will look at the mirror

U see your face

U will see your heart

U will see your body

And u will not recognize it

Because u will be so used

Used from the rejection

Used from the loneliness

Used from the fake people

Used from the bad decisions

Without faith!!!

**Eva Petropoulou-Lianou** was born in Xylokastro, Greece. Initially she loved journalism and in 1994 she worked as a journalist for the French newspaper "Le Libre Journal" but her love for Greece won her over and she returned in 2002. She has published books and eBooks: "Me and my other self, my shadow" Saita publications, "Geraldine and the Lake elf" in English - French, as well as "The Daughter of the Moon", in the 4th edition, in Greek - English, Oselotos publications. Her work has been included in the Greek Encyclopedia Haris Patsis, p. 300. Her books have been approved by the Ministry of Education and Culture of Cyprus, for the Student and Teacher library.

# Antje Stehn

## Threshholds

Never underestimate

the tiny space between private and public

that threshold, that precise point

where conflict concentrates

where voices shout out for freedom

where women let their hair

blow freely in the wind

where young students

challenge batons and bullets

fighting to gain their dignity

to gain a life without gender apartheid

to gain life in peace

We stand at that threshold

and look out at our gardens

growing here long before us

long before the seeds of religion

before separating women from men

before all this killing

the garden was designed for tentacular climbers

who spread out their arms

toward the neighbors, the village

toward humanity

the garden was designed for

togetherness

**Antje Stehn**, member of German Exile-PEN, of the Italian Collective "Poetry is my Passion". She collaborates with the Piccolo Museo della Poesia, Italy and she is co-editor of the magazine TamTamBumBum. She has published five poetry Chapbooks. In 2022 her bilingual book Grotesque, Expeditionen Verlag, in 2024 her latest book Guerra. Since 2020 she is curating the art-poetry projects “Rucksack a Global Poetry Patchwork“, in 2023 “Hair in the Wind“ in solidarity with the Iranian movement "Woman, Life, Freedom" and in 2024 the antiwar project “The View of the other from a different point of yiew" which each involved more than 250 international poets. Her poems are translated into twelve different languages, published in many international anthologies and magazines.

# Stephen Kent Roney

## A Rumour of Lions

I fear I have already said too much;
This is a world where a stray word can cost lives.
Jackals roam the streets.
Long ago, they say, lions roamed the high places,
And they were dangerous.
The jackals said they would protect us.
But the lions were rare,
Prominent in the mountain light,
Clearly seen and kept apart;
Not in every alley like the jackals,
Sudden from the shadows and behind,
Concealed in clerics' robes.
They say the lions are now gone;
Like the innocent stories of childhood;
Devoured or else driven out by jackals.
I'm sure they are right
They are always right
I fear I have already said too much.

**Stephen Kent Roney** is widely published in Canada and abroad and winner of the 2021 Mensa World Poetry Prize. He currently resides in Saint John, New Brunswick, with a view of the sea.

# PJ Yukon

## Home

she'll grab you by the heartstrings
and never let you go
she's a haven for your heartbeat
and a heaven made of snow
she's a harbor where the midnight sun
never lets you down
and the blazing bright aurora
nails you to the ground

where the beaver slaps his happy tail
by the shores of an alpine lake
and the river runs right through ya
where the salmon clear the gate
where the moose calls out in the wilderness
to lure himself a mate
and the air is clear and the water here
is more than worth the wait

where you can walk across forever
and never see another soul
where the trails the moss and the tundra
ever beckon you to go
where the raven's laugh and the grizzly's roar
in the land of the midnight sun
will always leave you craving more
when a Yukon day is done

some call her a barren wasteland
some say she's a nowhere land
where it's 50 below and the ice and the snow

are unfit for the fittest man
some say she's an empty horizon
she's really no big deal
yet the gleam and the glow of the natural world
clearly say that the magic is real

some call her a wonder
some call her a drain
some wander and wonder
and wander again
but she'll get in your blood
like a verse of this poem
some call her the yukon
but i call her home

*This poem was made in The Yukon. And so was I.

Author's Note: Home. To me the word is sacred. I know what it's like not to have a home. Whether it's mansion, a hovel or a stack of sticks on a mountaintop somewhere in the Yukon – which I can relate to - it is a sacred place where your heart will always live. Amen. ©PJ Yukon 2024

# THIS IS NOT A HOLY WAR

this is not a holy war
this is not a holy war
this sanctionless massacre
by evil-altered minds
schooled in hate and greed
tutored in violence
led by monsters
and genocidal maniacs
who will support
even the burning of a child
in its bed

i was not
spoon-fed your propaganda
that says killing is ok
not brain-washed
to follow you mindlessly
as you ride on the coattails
of a mad man
bent on power
bent on oppression
bent on a tiny strip of land

where do the souls
of the children go
when they leave this world
limbs blown off
screaming in pain
their faces reddened
and shredded
by shrapnel

so that only god
can know them now?

where do the mothers go
when there is nowhere to go
when there is no home
no family
when far beneath
the guns
the tanks
and the rubble
lie the ravaged bones
of their children?

how can you sleep soundly in your bed
joke with your wife and children
when you break every law god made
is there anything so compelling
about a strip of sand that can justify
even the murder of a child
that stone you covet
was there long before you were
and it will be there
long after you are gone

yet forevermore
beneath these tarnished skies
below the guns the tanks and the rubble
lie the innocent souls
of the sons and daughters
who once lived here
now doomed to remain children
for eternity

now little more than a tear
in the eye of god

this is not a holy war



Author's Note: I take no political position. This was hard to write but I felt I had to write it. I object to the killing of innocent souls. There is no excuse. *Strong language.

**PJ Yukon**, Canadian poet PJ Yukon was invested as Yukon Poet Laureate in 19194. Known for her literary works and advocacy for animal welfare, particularly for sled dogs, she is the author of several books of poetry. Recognized for her contributions to Yukon arts and culture, she is known for her live performances and storytelling incorporating music and spoken words. Her works reflect her connection to the Yukon and its people. She is considered a prominent figure in Canadian literature.

# Kelly Kaur

## No More Bullets. No More Bombs

Strain to listen to the voices
Daughters, sisters, mothers, grandmothers
Innocent girls
fiery women

Silenced by the ricochet of bullets
Bombs shatter hope
Deafened by the unchartered chaos
Lives decimated in protests
Pain, persecution, death

Still
their spirits rise
Again
Again
Again

Through centuries
Through veils
Through beatings
Through ancient laws that govern

Lean forward
Eavesdrop
How freedom sounds
Close your eyes
See the shape of rebellion

When words gather hope
When power rebuilds in streets
Bullets rebound
Bombs vaporize

**Kelly Kaur** is a writer, author, and speaker. She was recognized at the Alberta Legislature for her writing and for honoring Punjabi Sikh heritage for her children's book, Howdy, I'm Singh Hari. She was awarded the 2025 South Asian Inspiration Award for Achievement in Arts and Culture (SAIA) and was a recipient of the Top 25 Canadian Immigrant Award in 2024. Kelly has a novel, Letters to Singapore, a poem on the Moon, and an upcoming poetry collection – My Love is a Durian. She's a reader for the International Human Rights Art Movement, New York, and a two-time TEDx presenter.

# Chris Wanamaker

## Last words of a revolutionary

Into the wilderness I will go
Into the desert I will walk
Onto the ice caps I will drop
Through the rain trees I will trek

Into the wilderness I will go
to the dungeons of the disappeared
and attics abandoned by ghosts
In the dust and dark let me decay
and turn
into skeleton
Let gas from a can spill
Let me be consumed by fire

I will climb to a crumbling peak
Dive from there into the deep
drown under the waves

Under the rubble I will lie
To the dark I will not surrender
Into the wilderness I will go

Let me be crucified!
nailed to a stake
and lowered
into a grave
Let me blend
into brimstone

*You may wonder* what lunacy lets me let you
take me
to the darkest corners of the cosmos
Why must I do this at all?

What is it that draws me, compels me toward
nothing?
not just a small nothing
but the big Nothing with a capital N?
What is it that calls me to zero, zilch, emptiness?
What kind of madness?
How did I become so deranged?

But it is not my choice
I do not have a say
An inner voice has whispered and now it shouts
"Into the wilderness you will go!"

And so, to our cause
I commend my spirit

The universe has cast its die
The cosmos has decreed my fate
I am willing
but the hour is late
Into the wilderness let me go

A retired clinical social worker and Anglican priest, in recent years **Chris Wanamaker** has created and hosted podcasts and radio shows featuring poets, fiction writers and political commentators. On these shows and at open mics he also shares his own poetry. He writes prose poetry in simple language that sometimes tells a story and uses imagery to convey movement and feeling.

Chris has lived and worked in many parts of Canada, including Canada's north, where he experienced life in small, cold, dark, isolated and insulated northern communities.

# Anne Sorbie

## Opposition

As Luna rises at the east end of
the Bow Valley, Sol faces her in the west.
Sun and Moon stare across the world at each
other. Between them, singing soft, are the
voices of murdered school children. Meanwhile
their grandmothers refract the glorious
sound for their weeping parents. The growing
dead, every one, somebody's girl child.

What kind of man pulls the trigger and bombs
a school to hedge the price of dirty oil?
Better he stays in his underground lair,
bunkered, with a detail counting dough rae
me, because one day soon the missing files
will be set on fire, and that pedophile
body will burn in its own hell.

**Anne Sorbie** is a writer Scottish born, Canadian writer. She has published four books, the latest of which is (M)othering, an anthology (co-edited with Heidi Grogan). Her work has appeared online at CBC Books, and in a range of Canadian magazines and journals.

One of her latest and deepest commitments is advocating for folks in long term care.

As an act of social protest, Anne is currently writing about love and hope

# George Elliott Clarke

## Morality Police Manual (7th Edition): Foreword

There is no cure for congenitally seditious *Beauty*,
though it bewitches and bedevils,
deranges and disorients,
our jelly-fragile eyes
(those much too readily besmirched
or tears-and-dirt-muddied receptacles);
and mere *Man* cannot distinguish
between angel and whore—
even if the harlot is a daughter
or a wife
or even (regrettably) one's own mother.

Thus, our beneficent and faithful State
avails itself of an up-close-and-personal *Sadism*,
a touchy-feely and child's-play-corrective *Sadism*,
that restrains, re-educates, reproves
only the malicious bitches communicating
*Blasphemy*,
for only these incorrigible *femmes fatales* require
*Sturm-und-Drang* buffeting recalling
the excruciating tactics
of the Yankee-trained SAVAK of *l'ancien régime*,
i.e., to put boots to a belly,
to stomp out a fetus,
to behead an adulteress….

Gentlemen and officers, your duty is delicate.

For instance, you may find, in prosecuting
succubi and incubi,
i.e., inescapably manhandling them, fondling them
(chests, thighs, buttocks)—
due to their absolute wriggling—
their resolute wiggling—
that you suffer instant, rapacious *Arousal*,
or even experience a debonair thirst
to suckle on stripped bare breasts,
thus imperilling your orderly execution
of confinement, tortures, and humiliations.
Recognize that you are thus enthralled,
spellbound by the wily, beguiling, unrepentant,
and unpredictable whore.
In such cases, and we speak warningfully,
you are obliged to cut off the viper's head
or slice off the bovine udders,
so as to preserve your own *Sanctity*,
and remain thus perfectly immune to State
*Oppression*.

Remember, dear sirs:
Our State is *Nature* regimented;
plus *Human Nature* purified;
in our blessed domain, the satanic worm
cannot infect or devour the unblemished rose.
Therefore, we raise high our veritable gloves
to wipe away spiritual scum
or thrust backsliders, sprawling, spread-eagled,
into vile muck—
the wretched, stenching sty—
or the sulphurous, fuming, subterrain *abbatoir*.

So, let your shirtsleeves proudly protrude iron fists—
*de rigueur* hammers—
and let *Hatred* solidify your hearts to toxic lead:
How else will you trample vermin?
Let no one misinterpret your *Outrage*,
that you reject paralyzing, black-widow *Beauty*,
that you will crush
the woman who is Jezebel,
the girl who is Medusa!

It is better to banish their faces—
to disappear their hair—
than fall prey to their visages
posing as seductive overtures to hellacious *Blasphemy*!

Remember that *Beauty* is transcendentally treasonous,
a frank brutality to the perfection of *Scripture*,
and that our born foe—the female—
is capaciously specious, vicious, atrocious,
and—alas—disarmingly luscious.

But do not pander to her!
Do not let her looks sully your eyes!

Your duty is to sterilize the society,
to prevent the female's monthly blood
from ferrying septicemia or ebola,
venereal malaria or bastardy.

Only the Morality Police can prevent

the prolific propagation of infidels,
those who beget lice and worship maggots.

Finally, if you do find yourself overwhelmingly
muddled
by a temptress, a slut,
and feel that you must use
*even a girl-child—*
have her, take her,
and then put the defiling creature away,

lest your *Purity* be fatally contaminated.

The 4th Poet Laureate of Toronto (2012-15) and the 7th Parliamentary/Canadian Poet Laureate (2016-17), George Elliott Clarke was born in Windsor, Nova Scotia, in 1960. An English prof at the University of Toronto, Clarke has taught at Duke, McGill, UBC, and Harvard. Laurels? Pierre Elliott Trudeau Fellows Prize, Governor-General's Award for Poetry, National Magazine Gold Award for Poetry, Premiul Poesis (Romania), Dartmouth Book Award for Fiction, Eric Hoffer Book Award for Poetry (US). *Basta!*

# Mansour Noorbakhsh

## debris

i engrave your name
slowly
and after each scratch
i gently blow the debris
and cover the letters with my hand
turning my eyes around like a thief

i engrave your name
on a wooden bench
where we have never seated together

where have you scratched my loneliness
where have you blown its debris?

## Roots

There are no obstacles for roots.
Roots know how to crack the stones.
Or to pierce the walls.
Even the walls of prisons
which are guarded strongly.

## Change

If you find me one day unchanged, stagnant, still.
Never admire me for being consistent.
Hate me. Leave me alone and don't justify the state of my existence.
Nor do lionize me to make a sudden leap.
Till I return to you somewhere different than where you left me.

The stagnant water should be vaporized by sunlight.
Or becomes absorbed by the earth.
To return one day pure and different.

**Mansour Noorbakhsh**, author of "In Search of Shared Wishes", "Till You Recognize Me", and "Powdery Wings". He has presented "The Contemporary Canadian Poets" and "The World Poets" in a weekly Persian radio program from 2020 to 2024.

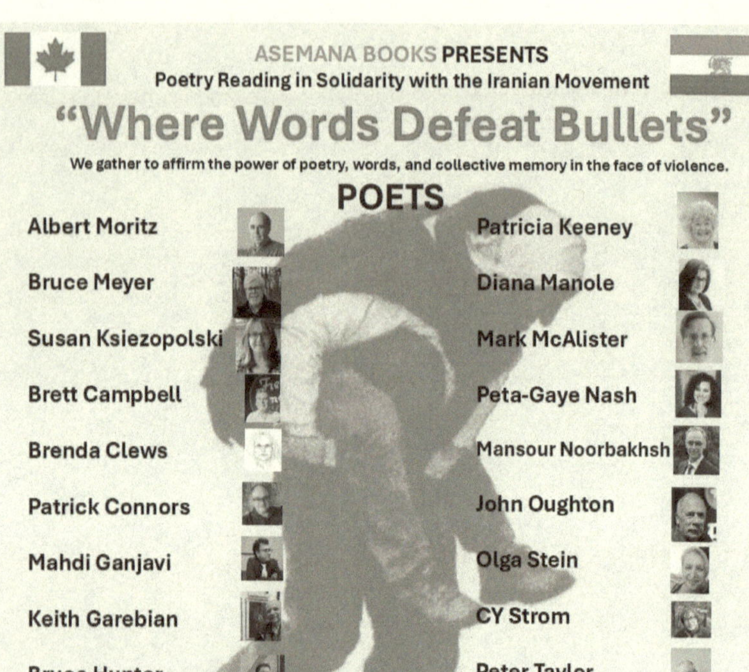


Flyer for the *Where Words Defeat Bullets* event, organized by Asemana Books and hosted by Mansour Noorbakhsh.

A photo taken after the *Where Words Defeat Bullets* event, organized by Asemana Books, featuring the poets.

# Asemana Books

*Devoted to Publishing Diasporic, Underrepresented and Progressive Literature on the Middle East.*

Email: Asemanabooks@gmail.com
Webpage: asemanabooks.ca

## Scholarly and Academic Research

- *Iranian Solar Calendar and Endurance of Nowruz in Persian Time Culture* – Abbas Amanat – 2025
- *Theatre in Travel*– Duman Riyazi– 2025
- *Tanglusha of a Thousand Images: Essays on Culture and Literature* – Reza Farokhfal – 2024
- *Language, People, and Society: Iranian Minority Languages and Literary Traditions* – Edited by Amir Kalan, Mahdi Ganjavi, Anisa Jafari, Lale Javanshir – 2024
- *Music on the Borderland: Remembering and Chronicling the 1979 Revolution's Shadow on Iranian Music* – Keyan Emami – 2024
- *Implications of Class Analysis in Capitalist Imperialism* – Mohammad Hajinia and Shahrzad Mojab – 2024
- *Dark Night and Phoenixes of the Ashes: Nima Yushij's Poetry from 1932–1942* – Ramin Ahmadi – 2024
- *Whispers of Oasis: Likoo's Poetic Mirage* – Mahdi Ganjavi, Amin Fatemi, Mansour Alimoradi – 2024
- *Hafez and Irony* – Reza Farokhfal – 2024
- *Kurdish Women at the Core of the Historical Contradictions on Feminism and Nationalism* – Shahrzad Mojab – 2023
- *The Peasant Uprising of Mukriyan 1952–1953: Consulate Documents, Diplomatic Correspondence, and the Press Coverage* – Amir Hassanpour – 2022

## Memoirs

- *Adventures of Pen and Lens*– Reza Allamehzadeh – 2026
- *Colour and Mystery*– Irene Monique Salehi – 2025

## Critical Edition

- *The Basil that Enlightens the Garden*– Mirza Agha Khan Kermani, edited by M. Rezaei Tazik – 2025
- *The Art of Speaking and Writing* – Mirza Agha Khan Kermani, edited by M. Rezaei Tazik – 2025
- *Creation and Legislation* – Mirza Agha Khan Kermani, edited by M. Rezaei Tazik – 2025
- *The History of Changes in Iran* – Mirza Agha Khan Kermani, edited by M. Rezaei Tazik – 2024
- *Rostam in the Twenty-Second Century* – Abdulhussain San'atizadeh Kermani, edited by Mahdi Ganjavi and M. Mansouri – 2017

## Poetry

- *The World Stares at Me. And I at Heart* – Bijan Safdari – 2026
- *My dreams breathe in broken fragments*– Hadi Ebrahimi Roudbaraki - 2026
- *Prism of Wounded Light* – Amin Haddadi, Translated by Dariush Shahinrad - 2025.
- *Shape of Extinction* – Poetry of Bijan Jalali, Translated by Adeeba Shahid Talukder and Aria Fani - 2025
- *One Hundred Nights of Yearning* – Mansour Noorbakhsh – 2025
- *Songs of Barbad* – Amir Hakimi – 2024
- *With My Shadows, I Created Myself* – Hadi Ebrahimi Roudbaraki - 2024
- *Citizens of September* – Saeid Rezadoust - 2024
- *Wonder of Memory* – Amir Hakimi – 2023
- *Galaxy Has No Memory of the Sunset* – Mahdi Ganjavi – 2023
- *Strangers Who Live in Me* – Mahdi Ganjavi – 2021
- *Exiled to the Rocky* – Ali Fatolahi – 2018

## Fiction & Plays

- *The Qualities of Children That We Thought Were Stronger Than Bombs*, a novel by Siamak Vossoughi, 2026
- *Our decline*, a novel by Peyman Yarian, 2026

- *The Blue Side of the Sky*, a novel by Javad Alavi, 2026
- *Badri*, a novel by Behrooz Badakhshan, 2025
- *My Husband, My Feather Pillow*, a novel by Fatemeh Zarei, 2025
- *Destined to Lead?* - a novel by Hushand Dowlatabadi, translated by Hadi Dowlatabadi, 2025
- *56 Degrees*, a novel by Hossein Noushazar, 2025
- From The Northwest, short stories by Amirhossein Bakhtiari, 2025
- *An Iranian Odyssey* - a novel by Rana Soleimani, translated by Fereidon Rashidi, 2025
- *Family Secret Momories* - novel by Mohammad Qassemzadeh, translated by Mahshad Abdoli, 2025
- *Stories from Tehran* - short stories by Fereshteh Molavi, 2025.
- *Escape from the Girl's Complex* - Mahbobe Mousavi – 2025
- *Yousef, Joseph, Guiseppe* – Ali Foumani - 2025
- *An Iranian Odyssey* – Rana Soleimani – 2025
- *Lead to Evil* – Javad Alavi – 2025
- *We Are Drunk and Broken, and No One Is Witnessing Us* – Mahdi Ganjavi – 2025
- *Someone Had Died in Front of Our House* – Akbar Falahzadeh – 2024
- *Zinat* – Vahid Zarrabi Nasab – 2024
- *Siberian Crane* – Ali Foumani - 2024
- *Elephants Reached the Plain* – Kaveh Oveisi - 2024
- *Textual Mosaic* – Marzieh Sotoudeh – 2024
- *Expectations of a Dream* – Mahdi Ganjavi – 2020

Asemana Books is devoted to publishing diasporic, underrepresented, and progressive literature on the Middle East.

asemanabooks.ca

ASEMANA BOOKS

www.ingramcontent.com/pod-product-compliance
Lightning Source LLC
LaVergne TN
LVHW050957080826
845145LV00009B/2327

* 9 7 8 1 9 9 7 5 0 3 4 1 5 *